God's Plan of Salvation

Understanding the Story of the Bible

By

F.B. Gold

© 2023

Contents

Chapter 1: Introduction

Chapter 2: God Creates (Genesis 1-2)

Chapter 3: Sin Spoils Everything (Genesis 3)

Chapter 4: God Calls Out a People of His Own (Genesis 12)

Chapter 5: God is Holy & Merciful (Deuteronomy 6)

Chapter 6: God Promises an Eternal King (2nd Samuel 7)

Chapter 7: The Messiah Will Be a Suffering Servant (Isaiah 53)

Chapter 8: The Messiah Arrives (Luke 1-2)

Chapter 9: Jesus Dies (John 19)

Chapter 10: Jesus Lives & the Holy Spirit Indwells (Luke 24)

Chapter 11: God's Perfect Kingdom (Revelation 20-22)

About the Author

Chapter 1: Introduction

"I've been quite staggered to find out how many people of great significance and worth, both as Bible teachers and as theologians, clearly have 2nd Samuel 7 in the very heart of their top ten list of most significant chapters of the Bible."

I remember furrowing my brows when I heard the pastor make that admission. It was sometime in 2022, and I was listening to an Alistair Begg sermon-podcast. His statement caused me to pause, not necessarily due to disbelief – for over the years he had earned my trust – but rather because I'd simply never realized that Bible scholars considered the seventh chapter of 2nd Samuel to be so important. John 3 or Romans 8, sure, but 2nd Samuel 7? If it is so significant, then why don't preachers reference it more often in their sermons? While I'd personally read through the book of 2nd Samuel a couple of times before on my own, I am positive that podcast was the first time I'd ever heard someone actually preach on that specific chapter. Not only that, but of all the verses that I'd ever heard people quote or had read on t-shirts, coffee mugs and bumper stickers, I was confident that none of them had come from 2nd Samuel 7. And I'd certainly never memorized any verses from the chapter myself. So, this information was a bit staggering for me, as well. Pastor Begg would continue.

"In fact, it would be fair to say that what we have here in this chapter is not simply the key to understanding all of 1st and 2nd Samuel, as it is, but in actual fact, here in this chapter you have a key which unlocks the entire storyline of the Bible."

2nd Samuel 7 is one of the keys to unlocking the entire storyline of the Bible? Now, that was a bold statement. Not surprisingly, though, Pastor Begg was able to back up his claim, and afterwards, the sermon stuck with me, causing me to do some introspection. First, I wondered, if someone asked me, could I adequately explain to them the storyline of the Bible? Heck, was I even sure that I knew what the storyline of the Bible was? And, secondly, what would I determine to be the top ten most significant chapters of Scripture? I had never before considered those questions.

    Jump forward about a year. My mother and I had been conducting various studies together over the course of several months where we would choose a book of the Bible at random and go through each of its chapters a week at a time. We'd just finished the book of Ruth, and she'd asked what we should study next. I remembered the Alistair Begg sermon and recommended that we try something different. How about telling the story of the Bible and doing so by focusing on only ten chapters? After pondering it further, I realized my proposal would be too difficult for me. So, instead of just ten chapters, I changed it to ten passages. That would allow me to 'cheat,' so to speak, by combining two or more chapters together and considering them to be a single passage. She agreed to the idea, and somewhere along the way, I sensed God encouraging me to post my thoughts online with the hope of sharing the study with those who are not familiar with the Holy Scriptures – be they atheists, agnostics, or even new believers. People who, perhaps, are interested in learning more about God's Word but find the prospect of reading the entire book too daunting. I truly doubt if anyone will actually read this study, but regardless, I am publishing it in obedience to His leading.

    Obviously, the first step in the study was to determine what I thought was the single, overarching story of the Bible. Only after making that determination could I then pick the ten passages that would help me to tell that story. God's Word consists of sixty-six separate books or letters, written by around forty different human authors over a span of about fifteen hundred years. Or, at least, that's one perspective. The apostle Paul, in writing to his protégé, Timothy, states, *'All Scripture is God-breathed...'* (2 Timothy 3:16). Meaning that the Bible is really only one book with one author – God Himself – with a single, unifying narrative that threads its way from the beginning to the end. And, ultimately, I believe that narrative is about God revealing Himself and His glory to the world. Therefore, I could have entitled this study, "The Glory of God," and it would have been quite accurate. That said, I believe that the way God reveals His glory to the world is through showing us His characteristics – His power, His wisdom, His holiness and righteous justice, and certainly His mercy, love, and grace. And what is the primary way that He displays all of those characteristics? I believe it is through His plan of salvation. Therefore, I will be focusing on and explaining that plan in the chapters that follow.

Because this study will be a 'big picture' survey of the Bible, that means I will obviously be skipping many wonderful books of Scripture. Books that contain incredible stories and profound wisdom. Additionally, this study will not expound numerous, foundational Biblical doctrines – God's teaching on sex, the role of suffering in the life of a Christian, the purpose of the ordinances, just to name a few. Even within the ten passages that I have chosen to examine, I will not be discussing every verse. I will only be commenting on verses that clearly tie in to the Bible's overarching story, which, again, I believe is the story of God's grace-filled plan to save His children from their sins specifically through the person and works of His Son, Jesus. And since that is the unifying narrative, that means we will be able to 'glimpse' Jesus even before He ever stepped down from Heaven and into our world, for He – and the salvation that comes through Him – is routinely foreshadowed throughout the Old Testament writings. Indeed, the entire Bible is ultimately about Jesus. There is a maxim which states: in the Old Testament, Jesus is predicted; in the Gospels, He is revealed; in the book of Acts, He is preached; in the epistles, He is explained; and in Revelation, He is expected. I hope to show that in this study.

Before moving on to the next chapter, however, I would like to take care of a few 'housekeeping' items:

1. In this study, I will be using two different translations of Scripture – both the NIV (New International Version) and the ESV (English Standard Version). I have also italicized the Scripture to clearly differentiate God's Word from my thoughts. I don't want there to ever be any confusion on the two. Additionally, any time you see any words or phrases of Scripture underlined or if there are any non-italicized words found in brackets, please know that those were added by me in order to either emphasize or clarify a point.

2. I must mention that much of my knowledge and understanding of the Bible has been aided greatly over the years by reading books and listening to sermons by preachers and theologians much more learned and intelligent than I am. Men such as John Calvin, Charles Spurgeon, R.C. Sproul, Alistair Begg, Charles Swindoll, and Stan Britton. If you find anything useful in this study, most likely it came from one of them, for I am just an ordinary follower of Jesus doing my best to understand and obey His Word. I have never even taken any kind of Bible-study course much less graduated with a degree from a seminary. The point being, if there are by chance any errors in this study, then the blame lies entirely with me and not with the men I acknowledged above.

3. Finally, please know that this study should in no way replace the actual reading of the Scriptures. Reading my or anyone else's commentary about the Bible will not ultimately change your life. At best, it will only give you a little head-knowledge. It is only through the reading of God's Word itself or by hearing it preached that God, by the power of His Spirit, saves and transforms lives. My hope is that, by going through this study, you will be motivated to dig into the Bible for yourself and, in doing so, you will discover God's majesty and the beauty of His life-giving love.

Chapter 2: God Creates (Genesis 1-2)

The Bible begins with this statement: *In the beginning, God created the heavens and the earth.* (Genesis 1:1)

The writer of Genesis – and most theologians believe it to be Moses – didn't start his written account with any arguments in the field of apologetics. He doesn't provide any proofs on the existence of God. He doesn't get into any imaginary debates with atheists or try to persuade his readers against the validity of any scientific theories – be they the Big Bang theory or the theory of human evolution. [As a side note, since this writer felt no need to defend the existence of God, I will not do so now either. While I do believe that apologetics – that is, the branch of theology that is concerned with defending or proving the truth of Christian doctrines – has its value, I will not be exploring that topic here for it is not the purpose of this essay.] On the contrary, the writer starts with a simple, straight-forward – but incredibly profound – statement. In fact, I'd argue that this verse – and the others found in this first chapter of Genesis – contains *the* foundational truth of not only the entire Bible but also of the entire history of humanity. The claim found in this first verse is crystal clear: there is a God who exists outside of our time-space continuum. If the claim in Genesis 1:1 is not true – if, indeed, there is no God – then the rest of the Bible is absolutely meaningless. All of it. The veracity of all Scripture hangs on whether the God of the universe actually exists. Therefore, to understand – and more importantly to accept – the story of the Bible, then one has to accept the premise that there is a God.

However, the writer doesn't simply claim that there is a God and stop there.

Verses 3-5 state: *And God <u>said</u>, 'Let there be light,' and there was light. God <u>saw</u> that the light was good, and He <u>separated</u> the light from the darkness. God <u>called</u> the light 'day' and the darkness He called 'night.' And there was evening, and there was morning – the first day.*

The writer makes it clear that this God is not some unthinking, cosmic power. This God is not an impersonal karma or some magical Force, as found in the movie, Star Wars. Instead, the Bible says that God created. He said. He saw. He separated. He called. These are all acts of an entity that has agency, a volitional will. Therefore, God is an intelligent being, one who purposefully created everything, including humans.

So, God created mankind in His own image, in the image of God, He created them; male and female He created them. (Genesis 1:27)

In the first paragraph, I claimed that the verses in Genesis 1 are foundational to understanding the history of humanity, and here is why. God didn't just create the sun and moon and constellations, nor just the mountains and plains and oceans. He also created mankind. He is the Author of life. This is vitally important because it tells us – humanity – that we are not here by accident. We are not simply the result of time plus matter plus chance. We did not randomly spring forth from some sort of primordial sludge. On the contrary, God *intentionally* created us. This truth grounds us because it tells us where we come from and how we got here. It begins to answer those deep, existential questions that virtually all humans ask themselves at some point in their lives. "Where did we come from? Who am I and why am I even here? Is there any meaning to life at all? Where am I going?"

However, the declaration in Genesis 1:27 goes deeper than simply telling us of our origin. The writer states that not only did God create us, but He created us in His own image. The all-powerful, all-knowing, perfect, holy God of the universe crafted us in His own image. To this day, I still can't truly get my mind wrapped around that. Now, there is some debate amongst theologians on what exactly 'being in God's own image' means, but what can't be argued is that it makes us unique. We – humans – are the pinnacle of God's creation. Nowhere else in chapter one of Genesis do we read that God crafted any of His other creatures in His own likeness. And since we humans were originally created in the image of God, that is why we have inherent value. In some amazing way, we reflect God and His attributes, and that is why human life matters, because God matters. Now, our reflection of Him is incredibly marred – like a cracked mirror – but we won't get to the explanation of why that is until the upcoming chapter.

The next verse confirms that we humans are God's special creation.

God *blessed them* [the male and the female] *and said to them, 'Be fruitful and increase in number; fill the earth and subdue it. Rule over the fish in the sea and the birds in the sky and over every living creature that moves on the ground.'* (Genesis 1:28)

There are multiple implications found in this verse, including the manner in which we are to steward the earth, but I'm not going to explore those issues here and now. The important point is that God created mankind to be in a relationship with Himself. He is not an impersonal, far-off, emotionally-distant deity. In these initial chapters – and in truth, throughout the entire Bible – we see God blessing and speaking with – that is, having a relationship with – His human creations.

The final verse of Genesis 1 states: *God saw all that He had made, and it was very good.* (Genesis 1:31)

God's creation – His original creation – was not just 'very good.' It was perfect. It was heaven on earth. And chapter two of Genesis telescopes in on the creation of Adam and Eve – the first two humans – and confirms this 'goodness.' After putting Adam in the Garden of Eden to work it and take care of it (Genesis 2:15), *'The LORD God said, 'It is not good for the man to be alone. I will make a helper suitable for him.''* (Genesis 2:18) Chapter two ends with the writer stating, *'Adam and his wife were both naked, and they felt no shame.'* (Genesis 2:25)

This nakedness wasn't just a physical nakedness. It was an emotional and spiritual nakedness as well, which implies total intimacy. There was nothing between the man and his wife. No emotional hang-ups or insecurities, no deceit or fears came between them. They were in perfect intimacy with each other and with God.

At that point, Adam and Eve were God's people, in God's place, under God's rule, enjoying God's blessing. And, therefore, all that God had made was 'very good.' And that is because God is good. There is no evil found within Him. Not even a hint of darkness. And that's where chapter two of Genesis ends.

Now, anyone with a working brain and who has experienced any life at all will naturally ask, "If God's creation was so 'very good,' then how did we end up where we are?" And that is a reasonable question. Because, while 'good' can still be found in the world, no one can legitimately argue that it's not also full of hatred, violence and prejudice and hardships, sorrow, and pain. The world is full of death. So, if God is so good and if He is all powerful – so powerful that He can simply speak the universe into existence – then why is His creation the way that it is? That is an incredibly common question and one that I even asked on multiple occasions throughout my life – particularly before Christ saved me. Well, Genesis 3 answers that question. It is the next important step in the story of the Bible, and we will discuss that in the next chapter.

Chapter 3: Sin Spoils Everything (Genesis 3)

When we left Adam and his wife, Eve, at the end of Genesis 2, they were in the Garden of Eden experiencing perfect intimacy with one another, with God, and with the natural world around them. The Creator had given them free rein throughout the land, permitting them to rule over and enjoy its flora and fauna, with one exception. God told Adam, *'You are free to eat from any tree in the garden; but you must not eat from the tree of the knowledge of good and evil, for when you eat from it you will certainly die.'* (Genesis 2:16-17). Now, why was the fruit from this particular tree forbidden? Additionally, since it was forbidden, then why did God even put the tree in the garden in the first place? Well, the Bible doesn't say. In fact, there are many questions the Bible doesn't answer. One truth I have learned since becoming a follower of Christ is that, while the Bible tells us everything that we *need* to know with regards to who God is and how He plans to reconcile us back to Himself, it doesn't tell us everything we *want* to know. There are numerous questions and topics not addressed in the Bible that will remain mysteries on this side of Heaven. Additionally, there may be some who are reading this right now who question why God gets to decide the 'rules' at all. The answer to that is simple. Since God created all, then that means He owns it all. As the Psalmist states, *'The earth is the LORD's and everything in it, the world, and all who live in it; for He founded it on the seas and established it on the waters.'* (Psalm 24:1-2) Therefore, God is the sovereign ruler over everything, the supreme authority. We may not like His decrees and commands. We may rebel against them, but it is His right – as the Creator God of the universe – to decide what is 'right' and what is 'wrong.' With all of that said, the main point I'm trying to make from this verse is that God gave Adam and Eve one simple command. Just one restriction. That's all. All they had to do was to trust in God's wisdom and goodness. To trust that He not only knew best but that He also had their best interest at heart. As long as they trusted God and obeyed that one command, then they would continue to enjoy His blessings. Seems pretty simple. Except that there was an enemy in their midst.

Now the serpent was more crafty than any of the wild animals the LORD God had made. He said to the woman, 'Did God really say, "You must not eat from any tree in the garden?"' (Genesis 3:1)

A talking serpent suddenly appears in the story with zero details of who he is or where he came from. Is it a literal serpent possessed by a dark spirit, or is the writer using poetic imagery? I'm not one hundred percent certain. Again, the Bible doesn't tell us everything that we want to know. The apostle John, in Revelation 12:9, refers to the serpent as the devil, and as we shall soon see, he is clearly an enemy both to God and to Adam and Eve. All we can safely conclude from the text is that, at some point after God had finished crafting His perfect creation, evil entered the scene. And notice that the first thing the serpent did was go to the woman and question her about God's command. "Did God really say that?" he asked her. Also notice that he didn't even repeat God's command correctly. For the evil one loves to cast doubt on God's goodness and wisdom and to stir up confusion amongst God's people.

Eve replied, *'We may eat fruit from the trees in the garden, but God did say, 'You must not eat fruit from the tree that is the middle of the garden, and you must not touch it, or you will die.''* (Genesis 3:2-3)

Notice that Eve is in partial error with her answer. According to God's command found in Genesis 2, He never told them that they couldn't touch the tree. Only that they must not eat from it. So, it seems as if the serpent's ploy is already working.

'You will not certainly die,' the serpent said the woman. 'For God knows that when you eat from it, your eyes will be opened and you will be like God, knowing good and evil.' (Genesis 3:4-5)

Here, the serpent flat out lies to Eve. Before, he seemed to be just trying to cause confusion and stir up doubts, but now, he is clearly trying to deceive. In essence, he is telling Eve that God is a liar and can't be trusted. Not only that, he then makes a promise to Eve about what she will receive if she disobeys God. He tells her that she will be like God, which is ironic, since in the previous chapter we already read that God had created Adam and Eve in His image. Therefore, they were already like God. They were pure, without sin. But that wasn't enough for Eve.

When the woman saw that the fruit of the tree was good for food and pleasing to the eye, and also desirable for gaining wisdom, she took some and ate it. She also gave some to her husband, who was with her, and he ate it. (Genesis 3:6)

The woman has now been tempted. The idea of being like God is firmly planted in her mind. But instead of seeking aid from either God or from her husband in order to help her battle her disobedient thoughts, she focuses on the temptation. She first looks at the forbidden fruit, and then she begins to lust after it, until eventually she succumbs to it. And not only her but her husband as well. They both decided that they no longer wanted to be under God's benevolent rule. They wanted to be rulers of their own lives instead. As a quick aside, let me say that Adam completely failed in his role as a husband here. Whether we like it or not, the Bible is clear that the husband is called to be the head of the family (see Ephesians 5). The husband is responsible for the well-being of his wife and children. However, Adam is totally passive in this scene. At no time do we see him taking on a leadership role by stepping between the serpent and his wife in order to protect her from harm. Of course, neither do we see Eve deferring to Adam at any point.

I can only imagine what they must have been thinking as they ate the fruit, but at least a part of it had to be intense anticipation. For they had been promised that they would become like God. Well, the next verse has to be one of the most anticlimactic sentences in all of Scripture.

Then the eyes of both of them were opened, and they realized they were naked, so they sewed fig leaves together and made coverings for themselves. (Genesis 3:7)

Really? That's it? The devil promised that if they sinned against God – that is, if they disobeyed His command, rebelled against His rule, stopped trusting in His goodness – then they would become like

Him. They must have anticipated that the mysteries of the universe would be opened up to them. They must have dreamt of obtaining divine wisdom and possibly even unfathomable power. Instead, all that happened was that they realized that they were naked. Talk about a let-down. But that's what sin always does. Sin always makes promises that it can't keep. Please don't misunderstand. I am in no way saying that sinful behaviors can't be pleasurable. If they weren't enjoyable, then we wouldn't be tempted to partake in them. But the pleasure that sin brings is always fleeting, and it always leaves the sinner in a horrible state. There is always a cost. Because, now, the intimacy between the man and his wife has been spoiled. Before, they were naked and felt no shame, but now, notice that the first thing they did was to cover themselves. There is now a barrier between them. And we're no different today. When we sin, the first thing we want to do is cover our shame and hope that no one finds out about it.

But their sin didn't just tarnish their relationship. As we shall see, it also spoiled their relationship with God.

Then the man and his wife heard the sound of the LORD God as He was walking in the garden in the cool of the day, and they hid from the LORD God among the trees of the garden. (Genesis 3:8)

Their sin – and the guilt and shame that came from it – caused them to want to hide from their Creator. The intimacy that they had shared with God has been shattered. What's more, look at just how foolish sin has caused them to act. They actually thought that they could hide from God behind some trees. As if the all-knowing God of the universe wasn't aware of their location. But that's what sin does. When we're caught up in it, we act like fools.

But the LORD God called to the man, 'Where are you?' (Genesis 3:9)

It's curious that God asked the man where he was. I already mentioned that God knew of their location. I could be wrong, but I think this was simply God's way of asking, "Why are you hiding?" Also, notice that, even though Eve is the one who was tempted and initially ate the forbidden fruit, it is to Adam that God calls out first. Again, I believe this is because Adam, as the husband, was responsible for his family. Therefore, God was going to speak to him first.

He answered, 'I heard you in the garden, and I was afraid because I was naked; so, I hid.' (Genesis 3:10)

This verse reveals so much about human nature and our plight, for this is the first instance that fear is ever mentioned in Scripture. But it won't be the last. In fact, throughout the Bible, we read of God repeatedly telling His people to 'fear not.' I've even read somewhere that, of all the imperatives found in the Bible, 'Do not fear' – or some variation of it – is the most common. It is commanded more often than 'Do not murder,' or 'Do not steal,' or 'Do not commit adultery.' Adam's sin had caused his relationship with God to be fractured. And when God is not the ruler of our lives – when we are not trusting in His sovereign goodness – then fear takes hold. Our world is full of people consumed with anxiety, and we see right here in this verse, from where it all comes.

And He said, 'Who told you that you were naked? Have you eaten from the tree that I commanded you not to eat from?' The man said, 'The woman you put here with me – she gave me some fruit from the tree and I ate it.' Then the LORD God said to the woman, 'What is this you have done?' The woman said, 'The serpent deceived me, and I ate.' (Genesis 3:11-13)

Notice that, when confronted by God with their disobedience, the man and the woman both immediately shifted the blame. Adam pointed his finger at his wife, and Eve pointed her finger at the serpent. Adam even went so far as to imply that it was God's fault. 'It was the woman that *you gave me*. It's her fault.' Adam was basically telling God that had God not made Eve, then he wouldn't be in this mess. Shifting blame – it sounds familiar, doesn't it? I've heard many people claim that the Bible is a meaningless book. That it is nothing more than an obsolete relic from the past. 'What could a book written thousands of years ago in a primitive culture possibly teach us today?' I used to think the very same thing myself. I believed that the Bible was nonsense and that Christians were fools to willingly enslave themselves to its rigid, oppressive teachings. But the reality is that the Bible is still relevant today because the truths and principles found in it are absolutely timeless. Cultures and societies may evolve. New economic theories and political ideologies may be introduced. Technology, medicine, and education all advance. But the human heart has never changed. Our inner being – our nature – is no different today than that of Adam and Eve. Their original sin was thinking that they knew better than God and looking to a created object for ultimate fulfillment instead of looking to their Creator. And we are no different today. Instead of focusing on God to satisfy the longings of our hearts, instead of focusing on Him as the source of our identity, security, and self-worth, we look to the created things of this world. And that list of functional 'gods' is virtually endless – whether it's sex, money, food, a career, relationships, shopping, hobbies, our bodies, the approval of others, etc. The human heart is an 'idol' factory, and we will find anything and everything to worship other than God, who is the only one truly worthy of worship. And when we're confronted with this idolatry, when we are accused of wrong doing, what is our first inclination? It is to shift the blame to someone or something else, just like Adam and Eve did. We don't want to be held accountable for our actions. And it's not even something we have to be taught. Little children – as young as three and four years of age – will automatically and naturally shift blame when they know they've done something wrong. So, I'll repeat – all these millennia later, the human heart is exactly the same.

When God hears of what happened in the garden, He decrees a series of curses. He first addresses the serpent, telling him that he will be cursed above all creatures and then states, *'And I will put enmity between you and the woman, and between your offspring and hers; he will crush your head, and you will strike his heel.'* (Genesis 3:15)

Most theologians believe that this verse is not simply a prophecy explaining why the vast majority of people fear and hate snakes. It is believed that God's promise here is actually the first foreshadowing of Jesus found in the Scriptures. The woman's offspring – some translations say 'seed' – is referring to Jesus, and on the cross, the evil one would 'strike His heel,' since Jesus' death caused Him severe physical pain and His separation from His Father caused intense emotional anguish. However, it is also at the cross that Jesus would defeat or 'crush the head' of Satan, sin, and death through His sacrifice. We will discuss Jesus and His death – both its purpose and consequences – in much greater detail in later chapters, but I thought it important to point out this first prophetic promise found here, veiled though it may be.

God then decrees a curse upon Eve – that she will experience pain during childbirth. Apparently, had she not sinned, then childbirth would be painless. However, God goes even further with His curse, issuing a consequence that I believe is much more damaging than any physical discomfort – though, I recognize, as a man, that is easy for me to claim.

'Your desire shall be contrary to your husband, but he shall rule over you.' (Genesis 3:16)

This verse explains why relationships – particularly those between a husband and his wife – are so difficult and why the world is plagued by divorce. As I mentioned before, whether we like it or not, the Bible is clear that the husband is to be the head of the family. However, I would argue that many, if not most, women fight against that teaching, refusing to play the complementary role that God designed for them. And the reason is that most women have bought into the faulty worldview that a subservient role automatically equates to having a lesser worth. But that belief – that one's position is synonymous with one's value and dignity – is simply not true. It's certainly not Biblical. Anyone who has ever been a part of a sports team can attest to the fact that, while the players may hold a subservient role to the coach, they are just as valuable – if not more so – than the entire coaching staff with respect to the team's success. And a family is no different. But it is not just the women who are to blame for so many relationships failing. Husbands are just as guilty, for I'd argue that most men do not handle the role of leadership well, typically falling into one extreme or the other. Most husbands are either authoritarian in their leadership, creating a marriage filled with tyranny and oppression, or they act in a passive, spineless manner, completely abdicating their God-ordained role within the family. Earlier we saw Adam not being a leader by stepping between the serpent and his wife, and there were severe consequences for his failure. And for anyone thinking, "Eve didn't need any man to save her," my only answer is, "Look at the text. She clearly did." The bottom line is that when members of a family – be it the husband and father, the wife and mother, or the children – refuse to fulfill the role that God has designed for them, then chaos and division ensues.

After addressing the serpent and Eve, God finally turns His focus to the man. Because of Adam's sin, God informs him that the earth itself will now be cursed. Instead of living in a garden paradise, man will reside in a land full of thorns and thistles. And, while the text doesn't specifically state this, I believe it is safe to assume that this original sin is also the cause of droughts, floods, and all the other natural disasters that we now suffer. Our broken world stems from this curse caused by man's sin. Additionally, work – which had been enjoyable for Adam while living in the garden – would now be cursed, as well. And finally, God addresses what He had promised to Adam in Genesis 2:17. He had promised Adam that if he ate the fruit from the forbidden tree, then he would surely die.

'By the sweat of your brow you will eat your food <u>until you return to the ground</u> since from it you were taken; for dust you are and <u>to dust you will return</u>.' (Genesis 3:19)

The implication here is that had Adam and Eve not sinned, then they could have lived forever within Eden, enjoying intimacy with God. And as their descendants, we have inherited their sinful natures and, therefore, their mortality. It is their disobedience to God that caused our bodies to be cursed. It is why we are plagued by cancers and other types of diseases. It is why we eventually wear out, break down, and die. Sin spoils everything. It spoiled Adam and Eve's relationship with God. It spoiled the relationship between themselves, and it even spoiled their relationship with nature itself.

As I have already mentioned, God is holy, perfect, and good. That means that He has integrity. He always keeps His word. He always follows through with His promises, whether they are promises of blessings or promises of discipline and judgment. And He was faithful to His promise here by cursing Adam and Eve with death, even though it wasn't an immediate death, which leads me to my next point. As I wrote in the first paragraph, the LORD is the sovereign God of the universe. It is His right to rule over it and, therefore, bring judgment upon any of His creation that rebels against Him. And because He is righteous and true, then we can always trust that He will be faithful to His promises. But it is also His prerogative as to *how* He wants to execute those promises, and usually, how He decides to carry out His plan is contrary to how we would expect. So, He could have killed Adam and Eve the instant that they disobeyed Him and that would have been within His rights. That would have been righteous judgment. Truthfully, it is what they deserved. But notice that He didn't kill them immediately. He actually showed them mercy in the midst of administering His justice by allowing them to continue to live – at least for a while.

Also, notice that when God informed them that they would certainly die, He wasn't just referring to a physical death. Their sin also brought about a spiritual death in that their fellowship with God was severed. And the reason it was severed is because God is holy. He is so holy that He cannot allow for sin to be in His presence. Sin separates us from God.

So, the LORD God banished him from the Garden of Eden to work the ground from which he had been taken. (Genesis 3:23)

Adam and Eve were no longer God's people, in God's place, under God's rule, and enjoying God's blessing. And if all of that wasn't bad enough, they had no way – in and of themselves – to ever restore that intimacy.

After He drove the man out, He placed on the east side of the Garden of Eden cherubim and a flaming sword flashing back and forth to guard the way to the tree of life. (Genesis 3:24)

There was now a barrier between humans and their Creator. A chasm between them and life – both eternal, physical life but also spiritual life. They were separated from God with no way – in and of themselves – to reconcile that relationship. And the Bible is clear that every human being that has walked the face of the earth – save One – is in this same predicament. We prove that we are both the physical and spiritual descendants of Adam every time we disobey God and break His holy decrees. We are born with sinful natures, with souls that are bent in towards ourselves and away from God. We were designed by God to be in a relationship with Him, but, due to our sinful nature, we are alienated from Him with no way of fixing that relationship ourselves. We, like Adam and Eve, are deserving of death. But it actually gets worse, for the Bible is clear that while our bodies may die, our souls are eternal (Matthew 25:46). Therefore, in our natural state, we are destined to be apart from God for eternity. And that is what Hell is. It is the place where God is not. And if that is where the story ended, it would be a depressing story full of despair. But, as the title of this study claims, God has a plan of salvation. He has a plan to reconcile those who are alienated from Him. A plan to redeem us out of our slavery to sin. And we get a foreshadowing of that plan near the end of the chapter.

The LORD God made garments of skin for Adam and his wife and clothed them. (Genesis 3:21)

Before banishing them from the Garden, God displayed an act of grace to Adam and Eve. The definition of grace is unmerited favor. So, God clothed them not because they deserved it, not because of anything good that they had done. He clothed them simply because He wanted to. That is one aspect of God's multifaceted nature – He is both loving and gracious. This clothing that He gave them seems like nothing but a simple act of kindness, but in reality, it is so much more. Don't forget that, after they had sinned against God and had their eyes opened to their nakedness, they were ashamed and sewed fig-leaves together to cover themselves. But in verse twenty-one, we see God covering them with animal skins. Why is this important? The covering that He provided was much better than the one they had attempted on their own, once again showing that His plans are always better than ours. And notice that the clothes were made from animals. Meaning that God killed some of His creatures in order to clothe Adam and Eve. Remember, prior to their sinning, everything was perfect in the garden. So, there was no death. Not for Adam and Eve nor for the animals. But in this verse, we see God intentionally shedding blood in order to cover over the guilt and shame that was brought about due to their sinful disobedience. This is a clear foreshadowing of the sacrificial death of Jesus on the cross, which is the center of God's plan of salvation. A plan that removes despair from our story and gives us hope. But that salvation won't come for a very long time in our story, and until then, sin and its tragic consequences will spread like wildfire, like weeds in a garden. We will look at that devastation in the next chapter.

Chapter 4: God Calls Out a People of His Own (Genesis 12)

In Genesis 3, we saw sin enter the story. Adam and Eve stopped trusting in God's wisdom and goodness. They decided that they knew better than their Creator and rebelled against His sovereign authority, disobeying His one command. The consequences of their sin were dire. Everything became cursed. Death – both physical and spiritual – came into the world, and they were banished from God's presence. They were no longer God's people, in God's place, under God's rule, enjoying God's blessings. And once they were left to their own devices, their situation went from bad to worse. The depravity of the human heart was unleashed, and sin began to spin out of control. In fact, it is only one chapter later in Scripture where we see the first murder taking place, with Cain killing his brother Abel. Over the next few chapters, thousands of years elapse, with each generation passing their poisonous 'gene' of sin onto the next until finally we read this sentence in Genesis 6, *'The LORD saw how great the wickedness of the human race had become on the earth, and that every inclination of the thoughts of the human heart was only evil all the time.'* (Genesis 6:5) What a powerful indictment of the human soul.

I want to pause here for a moment for I believe that we are at an important topic. The third chapter of the Bible – with the introduction of sin and its consequences – gives answer to the incredibly common question of, "Why is our world – expressed both in nature and in humanity – the way it is?" Over the course of my life, I have heard many atheists claim that one of the primary reasons that they don't believe in the existence of a god – and particularly in the existence of the God of the Bible – is due to the condition of our world. And if I'm honest, while I obviously don't agree with their conclusion, I can understand their point of view. I had similar thoughts prior to Christ saving me. They have been told – and rightly so – that God is all-powerful and all-loving, but then they look around and see a world full of injustice, suffering and death, and they conclude that those two facts are completely incongruous. The foundation of their rejection of God's existence lies on this premise: "If I was God, I would not allow little babies in Africa to needlessly die from AIDS. In fact, if I was God, there would be no suffering or hunger or oppression or death in the world at all." And since these atheists are not going to dismiss what they can clearly see – that is, the cursed world around them – then, in their mind, the only logical conclusion is to dismiss what they refuse to see – that is, a benevolent, all-powerful God. On a few, rare occasions, I've even heard professed atheists and agnostics strangely show tremendous anger towards the very God that they say they don't believe in, blaming Him for the brokenness of the world. I can honestly empathize with their frustration. What these people are not taking into account, however, is the holiness of God. People are very quick to believe in a God who is loving and merciful. I mean, who wouldn't like that? The idea of God as a kindly, forgiving grandfather is a very comforting thought. However, virtually no one wants a God who is the righteous Judge of the universe. But the Bible is clear – God is both. God is the all-loving and all-powerful Creator and, therefore, He did make the world perfect. In His original creation, there was no death, injustice, or suffering. But He is also the holy, righteous Judge who rightly condemned humanity for its rebellion against Him. As I mentioned in the last chapter, Adam and Eve deserved the punishment that they received. In fact, it is only because of God's mercy that they weren't put to death immediately. It is only God's mercy and kindness that the human race and this world exist at all. Therefore, who is to blame for the world being so broken? It is humanity. We humans are to blame. It is our fault that the world is the way it is, including the fact that little babies in Africa die of AIDS. But, as a whole, we don't want to accept that – and we certainly don't want to accept the idea of God as a holy Judge –primarily because we don't want to be held accountable for our actions. Just like Adam and Eve did when they sinned, we want to shift the blame. "The world's brokenness can't be our fault," humanity says. "In fact, we're fantastic and are doing our best to make the world a better place. Therefore, the condition of the world must be God's fault. It's either that, or there simply is no god, and we're nothing more than rudderless ships being tossed about by indifferent waves on a sea of chance. But make no mistake, it can't be our fault." Well, the Bible is clear – it is our fault. So, let's now move on and explore God's plan to save us from the mess we've made.

I am intentionally skipping over the details found in chapters four through eleven of Genesis, for as I've said before, this study will be only focusing on ten select passages. However, if you choose to read those chapters on your own, you can see a pattern emerge. It is a pattern that I already mentioned above with regards to Adam and Eve, and it's a pattern that we can actually see throughout the rest of Scripture. The pattern is this: in response to God's revelation of Himself to the world, humanity rebels against Him. In response to humanity's sin, God brings about holy judgment. However, even within that judgment, He still shows mercy to whom He wants to show mercy. So, it should be no surprise that at the end of Genesis 11, we see God once again bringing judgment upon humanity for their sinful pride by confusing the language of all the people and scattering them over the face of all the earth. (Genesis 11:9) But when we move into chapter twelve, we will see God's mercy and grace once again revealed.

Now the LORD said to Abram, 'Go from your country and your people and your father's household to the land that I will show you. And I will make you into a great nation, and I will bless you; I will make your name great, so that you will be a blessing. I will bless those who bless you, and whoever curses you I will curse; and all the peoples on earth will be blessed through you.' (Genesis 12:1-3)

Humanity had been scattered over all the earth, but out of that dispersion, God decided to call out Abram, who He would later rename Abraham, which most likely means 'the father of many.' To understand why this calling is important, I think that now is a good time to pause again in order to explain a framework that I will be using throughout this study. As we examine the story of God's plan of salvation, we will do so with the framework – or through the prism, if you will – of God's kingdom. For example, we can know that God's plan of salvation has finally been fulfilled when we see His kingdom come to ultimate fruition. In full transparency, this framework is not an invention of my own. The theologian Graeme Goldsworthy defined God's kingdom as God's people, in God's place, under God's rule, enjoying God's blessing, and that was how I described Adam and Eve's relationship with God while living in the Garden of Eden in Genesis 2. It's obviously not a complete or exhaustive description of God's kingdom, but I think it is a good template and one that I will be returning to throughout the rest of this Bible study.

With that framework in mind, we can see that, if God's plan of salvation involved establishing His kingdom, then He would first require a 'people.' This shows, once again, that God is not a far-off deity. He is a personal God who, though He does not need us, for some mysterious reason, desires to commune with us. Similar to how He walked in the garden in the cool of the day with Adam and Eve, He still desires an intimate relationship with His chosen people. So, out of the chaos found in the world, God decided to call out a people of His own who would willingly and lovingly submit to His rule.

But why did God specifically call Abram? The Scriptures don't actually say. The text gives us some details about Abram's origin and about his family – his father, brothers, and wife – but nothing is revealed about his character at this point in the story. We do not read in Genesis 11 or 12 that Abram was a special man of honor and courage or that he possessed any other attractive personality traits that would distinguish him from those around him. Nor do we read that Abram was a particularly pious man who was desperately seeking God. Therefore, and I could be wrong, I think God chose Abram simply out of grace. Abram was called out by God not because of anything that he had done, but simply because God's heart was set on Abram.

God didn't simply call out to Abram, though. He also made him a promise. He promised Abram that He would bless Abram, make his name great, and turn him into a great nation. More so, God even promised that 'all the peoples of the earth' would be blessed through Abram. I can only imagine what Abram must have been thinking. He must have been overwhelmed, not only that the God of the universe would even reveal Himself and deign to speak to him, but that God would also choose to bless him so abundantly. Abram must have been humbled and asked, "What did I do to deserve this?" That is certainly a question that springs to mind when I think of God's love towards me.

Take notice though that God's promise to Abram was not unconditional. It was tied to the command that God had given to Abram. Before the promise of blessings was given, God commanded Abram to leave his country, his family, and his home and to go to the land that He would show him. Therefore, God's promise of blessing was dependent upon Abram's obedience to God's command. This is a pattern we see throughout the Scriptures. God gives a command – be it to an individual or a group of people – and tells them that if they obey the command, then they will receive blessings. And if they don't, then things will go very badly for them. That's the first part of the pattern: God's command and His corresponding promise. The second part of the pattern deals with the person's response. Do they trust God – trust in His wisdom, goodness, and faithfulness – and therefore obey the command? Or do they not trust God and therefore disobey? We see this same pattern over and over in the Bible: God's Command and Promise followed by either Humanity's Obedience and Blessing or Our Disobedience and Curse. This sequence plays out in both the Old and New Testaments. It still plays out for us today. The Lord Jesus gives an invitation to all who would hear. *'Come to me all who are weary and burdened, and I will give you rest. Take my yoke upon you and learn from me for I am gentle and humble at heart, and you will find rest for your souls.'* (Matthew 11:28-29) Jesus gives us three commands in these two verses – to come to Him, to take His yoke upon ourselves, and to learn from Him – but in truth, it is really just one command. He is telling us to entrust our lives to Him. To bow down to Him as our Lord and Savior. And He promises that if we do so, then He will grant us rest for our souls. He has put that invitation out to the world. What is our response? Do I trust God and the promises found in His Word or do I not? Whether I realize it or not, whether it's on the forefront of my mind or only down in the subconscious recesses of my soul, it is a question that I ask myself every day when deciding to obey God or to go my own way, and it was a question that Abram had to ask himself. God, who apparently had just revealed Himself to Abram, was asking him to give up all the things that provided him with safety and security – his country, his people, and his father's household – and to go into an unknown land. As far as we know, Abram had never been to this strange land. He didn't know of what dangers might lie ahead. So, he had to ask himself this question, "Do I trust God? Do I trust that He can and will fulfill His promises?" That question is much easier to answer for those of us who are living today because we have a written record of God's faithfulness as found in the Bible. We can read that God has never failed to fulfill His promises. But, as far as we know, Abram had no such record.

To make Abram's decision even more difficult were the circumstances surrounding both Abram and his wife, Sarai. First, we discover that Abram wasn't a young man when he received God's call. The text states that Abram was seventy-five years of age. So, it wasn't as if he had the energy of youth and was ready to go off on some grand adventure. But, more importantly, at the end of the previous chapter, it is written, *"Now Sarai was barren; she had no child."* (Genesis 11:30) Therefore, Abram had to have asked himself, "How can God turn me into a great nation when I don't have any children and my wife is barren?" It is a legitimate question. For God's promise to Abram wasn't just difficult. Due to Sarai's infertility, it was impossible. At least it was from a human perspective. It would take a literal miracle for God's promise to be fulfilled. Abram and Sarai would never be able to fulfill it on their own, which brings us to another important point: only God can fulfill His promises. And as the next verse in the text shows, Abram believed that He would.

So, Abram went, as the LORD had told him, and Lot went with him. Abram was seventy-five years old when he departed from Haran. And Abram took Sarai his wife, and Lot his brother's son, and all their possessions that they had gathered and the people that they had acquired in Haran, and they set out to go to the land of Canaan. (Genesis 12:4-5)

What absolutely incredible faith that Abram displayed. Now, whether or not Abram was hesitant, whether or not he had his doubts, we don't know. The text doesn't say. All it says it that he obeyed, which implies that he ultimately trusted that God would be faithful to His word, no matter how impossible it may have seemed. I think it is important to notice that Abram's faith in God was not a purely academic exercise. He wasn't just giving intellectual assent to the existence of God and His trustworthiness. He didn't say, "Yes, I believe in you, God, but I'm going to stay here in Haran, living my life just as I had before." That is not true faith. When I read the Scriptures, I see that God's call is always a call to action. He never calls us to maintain the status quo. God's invitation into a covenant relationship with Himself and our obedience to that call will always transform us. It will obviously change how we view God and ourselves, but it will also change how we view the world and, therefore, how we live in it. It will change how we think about sex and marriage, about work and money, about hobbies and volunteering. It will change how we view everything. In fact, I will go so far as to say that, as a general rule, if my professed faith in the Lord has not changed me in some radical way, then it might be best for me to examine the legitimacy of my faith. So, no, Abram's faith didn't allow him to stay in Haran. It caused him to place himself, his family, and his future into God's mighty hand, which brought about actual change in his life. As the text states, *'So, Abram went, as the LORD had told him…and they set out to go to the land of Canaan.'*

We don't know how long it took Abram to finally reach Canaan, but it surely must have been many weeks or even months. I can only imagine what Abram must have been thinking during the trip. Did he ever start to question his decision to obey God? Did he ever start to have doubts in God's faithfulness? We don't know, but the text does tell us that, after arriving in Canaan, God spoke to Abram once again.

Then the LORD appeared to Abram and said, 'To your offspring I will give this land.' So, he built there an altar to the LORD, who had appeared to him. (Genesis 12:7)

Did God appear to Abram through a vision, a dream, or an angel? We don't know, but He clearly manifested Himself in some manner, and it makes sense that He would need to. For, remember, at this point in history, God had not bestowed either His written word or

His Holy Spirit upon His people. Thus, if Abram was going to understand who God was and what He wanted, then God was going to have to appear and speak to him in some fashion. But more important than the manner of God's manifestation were God's actual words, *'To your offspring I will give this land.'* After the long and probably exhausting journey from Haran, God encouraged Abram by speaking to him again and repeating His promise. It was God's way of saying, "I know that it's been a while, but your trip wasn't made in vain. I haven't forgotten the promise I made to you. Your long and arduous journey will be worth it." God reminded Abram that, even though he had no children and his wife was barren, God would somehow, miraculously grant him offspring.

And how did Abram respond? He built an altar to the LORD at that very location where God had appeared. An altar is both a place of worship and a place of remembrance. So, we see Abram – the man of faith – becoming a worshiper of God.

The remainder of Genesis reveals that God, indeed, kept His promise to Abram. Despite Sarai's advanced age and infertility, God made her eventually conceive. Abram – renamed by God as Abraham – and Sarai – renamed by God as Sarah – would have a son, Isaac. And from Isaac would eventually come the nation of Israel, consisting of millions of people. God made the impossible happen. He always overrules both the affairs of men and even the laws of nature to ensure that His kingdom promises are fulfilled. However, the LORD did make Abraham and Sarah wait for twenty-five years before He worked His miracle, and I specifically bring up that fact in order to make an important point, which is the distinction between the delayed or partial fulfillment of God's promises versus His ultimate fulfillment.

In a previous chapter, I stated that God – as the Creator of all – is the sovereign ruler over all. He has the right to make whatever plans and commands and promises that He wills. More so, His sovereignty also means that He has the right to control the execution of those plans, including the timing of them. So, if He wanted to wait a quarter of a century before blessing Abraham and Sarah with a child, then that was His prerogative. A particularly difficult lesson I have learned in my years of being God's servant is that His ways and His timing rarely match up with my desires. I prefer quick success and instant gratification, and I don't think that makes me unusual. As a general rule, none of us likes to wait. But God's timing is not ours. That's an important point to remember as we continue with this study of God's plan of salvation. We will see Him fulfilling His promises and establishing His kingdom in incremental steps and over very long periods of time. The truth is that, even to this day, He still has not ultimately brought about His kingdom in its final form, but we will discuss that topic more in the last chapter of this study.

The rest of the book of Genesis – and in fact, the rest of the Bible – is filled with incredible stories of Abraham and his descendants. Stories of God communing with His chosen people and ultimately protecting them from all manner of dangers. Stories showing Him fulfilling the first component of the kingdom framework: God's people. We will explore the other parts of that framework – in God's place, under God's rule, enjoying God's blessing – in the next chapter.

Chapter 5: God is Holy & Merciful (Deuteronomy 6)

I have made the claim that we can see God's plan of salvation being fulfilled through the establishing of His kingdom, and we have defined His kingdom as God's people, in God's place, under God's rule, enjoying God's blessing. In the previous chapter, we saw God fulfilling the first component of His kingdom by choosing a people of His own through Abraham and Sarah. In this chapter, we will explore God establishing the rest of His kingdom, and to do so, we are going to make a serious time-jump, moving from chapter twelve of Genesis to chapter six of Deuteronomy, the fifth book of the Bible. In full disclosure, I will touch on several verses found elsewhere, but chapter six will act as my starting point and home base.

In the book of Deuteronomy, well over five hundred years have passed since God first made this promise to Abraham, *"To your offspring I will give this land."* (Genesis 12:7) And during most of those years, the Israelites had lived as slaves down in Egypt. But at this point in the story, God's people are now just east of the Jordan River, on the cusp of finally entering the Promised Land. Before entering Canaan, however, God gives them some final instructions and reminders through His prophet, Moses.

'Now this is the commandment – the statutes and the rules – that the LORD your God commanded me to teach you, that you may do them in the land to which you are going over, to possess it, that you may fear the LORD your God, you and your son and your son's son, by keeping all His statutes and His commandments, which I command you, all the days of your life, and that your days may be long. Hear therefore, O Israel, and be careful to do them, that it may go well with you, and that you may multiply greatly, as the LORD, the God of your fathers, has promised you, in a land flowing with milk and honey.' (Deuteronomy 6:1-3)

We can see that God is finally going to bring His chosen people into the land that He promised them. They are finally going to be

God's people in God's place. More so, God, in His grace, is giving them a land that has already been tamed and cultivated. He's not bringing them into a land of thorns and thistles, so to speak, but rather into a land flowing with milk and honey. Therefore, we get a glimpse in the text of the fourth component of God's kingdom – enjoying God's blessing – as well. Moses reiterates this gracious act of God a few verses later.

'And when the LORD your God brings you into the land that He swore to your fathers, to Abraham, to Isaac, and to Jacob, to give you – with great and good cities that you did not build, and houses full of all good things that you did not fill, and cisterns that you did not dig, and vineyards and olive trees that you did not plant – and when you eat and are full, then take care lest you forget the LORD, who brought you out of the land of Egypt, out of the house of slavery.' (Deuteronomy 6:10-12)

Moses, the leader of the nation of Israel, is reminding God's people of God's faithfulness and His goodness. The Israelites had been oppressed and tyrannized for roughly four hundred years under the Egyptian pharaohs. But the LORD saved them out of that life of slavery, protected them from all manner of dangers as they traveled the desert for forty years, and finally, in His perfect timing, brought them to a land that was already filled with wonderful provisions. When I read these verses, I'm reminded of the Garden of Eden. When God brought forth Adam, He had already created the garden paradise in which Adam and Eve would live. Neither Adam nor the nation of Israel had to create the 'good things' which they would enjoy. God had already prepared those blessings for them in advance.

What is even more amazing is that God would show such kindness to the Israelites at all, for they were a people who in no way deserved such blessings. They were not special, in and of themselves. In fact, morally speaking, they were – like the rest of us – a very unrighteous and unpleasant group. Even after God redeemed them out of slavery, they constantly grumbled against Him, some of them even voicing their desire to be back in Egypt, the very place where they had been shackled in the chains of their oppressors. Moses reminds the people of their unrighteousness three chapters later.

'Know, therefore, that the LORD your God is not giving you this good land to possess because of your righteousness, for you are a stubborn people. Remember and do not forget how you provoked the LORD your God to wrath in the wilderness. From the day you came out of the land of Egypt until you came to this place, you have been rebellious against the LORD.' (Deuteronomy 9:6-7)

Can you actually imagine that? You have been saved out of an awful life of slavery, but afterwards, you're not satisfied with how your Savior is leading you. So, you grumble and rebel against Him, even going so far as to telling Him that you long to return to your former state of oppression. Unfortunately, I can imagine it. Every time that I disobey God, I am in essence telling Him that I prefer my old existence – being enslaved to sin – rather than enjoying the new life in which He has given me. Reading the Old Testament – especially about the rebellious nature of the people of Israel – is incredibly convicting because I see myself in them. I am – just as they were – truly unworthy of God's love and blessings. I am utterly amazed that God loves any of us. It is great mystery, but Moses explains how this can be.

'For you are a people holy to the LORD your God. The LORD your God has chosen you to be a people of His treasured possession, out of all the peoples who are on the face of the earth. It was not because you were more in number than any other people that the LORD set His love on you and chose you, for you were the fewest of all people, but it is because the LORD loves you and is keeping the oath that He swore to your fathers, that the LORD has brought you out with a mighty hand and redeemed you from the house of slavery, from the hand of Pharaoh king of Egypt.' (Deuteronomy 7:6-8)

How unfathomable is the kindness and patience of the LORD towards His people. He didn't choose them, save them, protect them, and bless them because they were a faithful and obedient people whose hearts were full of affection towards Him, but rather simply because His heart was set on them. He loved them simply because

He loved them, even though they didn't deserve it. How wonderful and amazing is our God.

So, from the verses that we've read, we can see that God's kingdom is about to be established. We have God's people, in God's place, enjoying God's blessing. But what about the third component of our definition – under God's rule? Most people don't want that part of the deal. Sure, they'll accept His blessings. Who doesn't enjoy blessings? But being under anyone's rule? No thank you. For the soul of every human is filled with rebellious pride and says, "I know what is best for my life, and no one is going to tell me what to do." But God – as the Creator – is the sovereign ruler of the universe. He rules over all – especially His chosen people – and we can see His rule from the text. Let's go back and re-read the first verses of chapter six, with emphasis added.

'Now this is <u>the commandment – the statutes and the rules</u> – that <u>the LORD your God commanded</u> me to teach you, that you may do them in the land to which you are going over, to possess it, that you may fear the LORD your God, you and your son and your son's son, by keeping all <u>His statutes and His commandments</u>, which <u>I command you</u>, all the days of your life, and that your days may be long.' (Deuteronomy 6:1-2)

The mentioning of all of these commandments, statutes, and rules brings us to a very important topic found in the Bible, a topic on which I am going to spend a bit of time – God's Law. It is sometimes referred to as the Mosaic Law since God gave it through His servant Moses. I am intentionally pausing on it because I think it is a subject that is very misunderstood, particularly its purpose. But before we get to the purpose of the Law, I feel the need to explain a little background.

After God redeemed the Israelites out of their slavery in Egypt, He led them to a mountain in the wilderness. At Mount Sinai, He brought Moses to the summit where He gave to Moses a list of commandments. The most well-known of them are referred to as the Ten Commandments. However, God's Law consists of more than these ten moral rules. If you go back and read Exodus, Leviticus, and Numbers, you will see that there are literally hundreds of commands found within God's Law, commands that cover virtually every aspect of life – laws concerning sex, marriage and divorce; very specific instructions on the proper worshiping of God; the rules of warfare; matters of justice and the legal system; the issues of economics; commands on hygiene and diet; and many more. The book of Deuteronomy is a retelling of many of these commands. In fact, the name 'Deuteronomy' is derived from the Greek for 'second law' and could be understood as 'a second telling of the Law.' So, before God's people entered the Promised Land, Moses was reminding them of God's authority and of His commands for them. But why did God give the nation of Israel these rules? For what purpose? There are actually several reasons, and I will attempt to go through each one quickly.

While the Bible itself does not differentiate between the various commands that are found within God's Law, over the centuries, theologians have done so. They have classified God's commands into three categories: the moral Law, the civil Law, and the ceremonial Law. They claim, for example, that the Ten Commandments explain how a person can be morally pure. On the other hand, the civil Law gave the people of Israel rules on how to live as a nation since, prior to entering the Promised Land, they had only lived as slaves. An example of a civil law would be the proper adjudication of a property dispute between two neighbors. And the ceremonial Law gave the Israelites instructions on how to properly worship God, including the crafting of the tabernacle and the Ark of the Covenant, the shedding of blood on altars, etc. Now, since God Himself, in His Word, did not categorize His commands, then I think it is vitally important to hold the idea of there being three different types of Law loosely. In the Bible, the Law is simply referred to as 'The Law.' At no point in Scripture is one of God's commands ever explicitly classified as being a particular type of law – moral, civil, or ceremonial. That said, I do believe that these three categories can help in explaining why the Law, as a whole, was given.

One reason I believe that the Law was given, based on my understanding of the Bible, was simply out of kindness by the LORD. God – despite what the majority of the world thinks – is not a great, cosmic kill-joy. He did not take His people out of one form of oppression – that is, slavery in Egypt – simply to subject them to another form of oppression through His commands. On the contrary, God loved His people, wanted what was best for them and, therefore, gave them some rules that would both protect them from harm and would enable them to flourish. God was treating His people like any loving parent treats his children. Loving parents don't let their children play in traffic, stay up late on school nights, or have a diet consisting of nothing but junk food. Instead, loving parents put rules in place to ensure the well-being of their kids. And God did the same. For example, in Deuteronomy 7:3, prior to His people entering the Promised Land, we read of God – through His prophet Moses – telling them, *'You shall not intermarry with them* [that is, the people already living in Canaan], *giving your daughters to their sons or taking their daughters for your sons....'* And why did God give this command? Again, it was for their good, as the next verse explains. *'...for they would turn away your sons from following me, to serve other gods.'* (Deuteronomy 7:4) As we saw with Adam and Eve, our lives go poorly when we turn from our Creator, and God doesn't want that for us so He put statutes in place to protect us. Moses confirms this fact at the end of chapter six.

'And the LORD commanded us to do all these statutes, to fear the LORD our God, for our good always, that He might preserve us alive, as we are this day.' (Deuteronomy 6:24)

He then repeats himself a few chapters later.

'And now, Israel, what does the LORD your God require of you, but to fear the LORD your God, to walk in all His ways, to love Him, to serve the LORD your God with all your hearts and with all your soul, and to keep the commandments and statutes of the LORD, which I am commanding you today for your good.' (Deuteronomy 10:12-13)

Therefore, it's plain to see that God gave His rules out of love, for the good of His people. But let's not misunderstand what that encompasses. God, like any good parent, also disciplines His children when they disobey the rules. Moses explains this fact to the people in chapter eight.

'The whole commandment that I command you today, you shall be careful to do, that you may live and multiply, and go in and possess the land the LORD swore to give to your fathers. And you shall remember the whole way that the LORD your God has led you these forty years in the wilderness, that He might humble you, testing you to know what was in your heart, whether you would keep His commandments or not. And He humbled you and let you hunger and fed you with manna, which you did not know, nor did your fathers know, so that He might make you know that man does not live by bread alone, but man lives by every word that comes from the mouth of the LORD. Your clothing did not wear out on you and your foot did not swell these forty years. <u>*Know then in your heart, as a man disciplines his son, the LORD your God disciplines you.*</u>*'* (Deuteronomy 8:1-5)

So, that is one reason the Law was given – because God is a wonderful Father who both blesses us and disciplines us out of love, for our good.

I believe that a second reason that God gave the Law was in order to display His holiness to the world and then, through that revelation, convict us of just how far we fall short of His perfect standard. God was clear with His people. He wanted them to be holy – that is, unlike the rest of the world. They were to be different. They were to be like Him.

And the LORD spoke to Moses, saying, 'Speak to all the congregation of the people of Israel and say to them, "You shall be holy, for I the LORD your God am holy."' (Leviticus 19:1-2)

So, to show the people of Israel what holiness looked like, God gave them the Law. In essence, God was saying, "I have called you to be holy, and here is my perfect standard." But, of course, no one can follow all of God's commands. At least, not perfectly. In fact, we can't even follow God's one primary command, as told by Moses to God's people.

'Hear, O Israel: The LORD our God, the LORD is one. You shall love the LORD your God with all your heart and with all your soul and with all your might.' (Deuteronomy 6:4-5)

Only one person who has ever walked this planet has ever loved the LORD with all of His heart and soul and might. All the rest of us have failed miserably. So, just like Adam and Eve, we can't even obey one of God's commands, much less all of the Ten Commandments or all of the other hundred statutes found in the Law. But here's the deal – God knows we can't. Just like He knew the Israelites couldn't. In fact, what follows is the message that God gave to Moses prior to His people entering the Promised Land. And, as you will see, God does not mince His words.

And the LORD said to Moses, 'Behold, you are about to lie down with your fathers. Then this people will rise and whore after the foreign gods among them in the land that they are entering, and they will forsake me and break my covenant that I have made with them.' (Deuteronomy 31:16)

That is truly mind-blowing to me. God knew that the Israelites were going to turn their backs on Him after settling in the Promised Land, and He let them enter anyway. The LORD – the all-knowing God – was fully aware that they would not keep His statutes because He knows well the depravity of the sinful, human heart. And Moses knew it, too.

And Moses summoned all Israel and said to them, 'You have seen all that the LORD did before your eyes in the land of Egypt, to Pharaoh and to all his servants and to all his land, the great trials that your eyes saw, the signs, and those great wonders. <u>But to this day, the LORD has not given you a heart to understand or eyes to see or ears to hear.</u>' (Deuteronomy 29:2)

In and of ourselves, we simply do not have the ability to seek after, to love, and to obey God. Our sinful hearts just aren't capable. We are, by nature, bent in towards ourselves and away from the LORD. And since that is the case, then it seems unfair for God to give a list of commands to His people that He knows they couldn't accomplish, doesn't it? Well, it would be unfair if the purpose of the Law was to act as a way for the Israelites to earn their salvation by showing God how righteous they could be. And, in my experience, that is what most people – even those who claim to read the Bible – think about the Law. They believe that God originally gave it to the Israelites as a way for them to achieve salvation, as a way for them to earn God's favor through their own righteousness. However, that simply cannot be, for the Law was given *after* God had already saved them out of slavery in Egypt. He had already set His heart upon them and shown them favor. Grace and salvation came first, then the Law was given. More so, the Law came several hundred years *after* God's initial promise to Abraham. God, out of grace, made a covenant with Abraham, promising to bless both him and, through him, all the nations of the world centuries before the Law was ever introduced. So, if the Law wasn't given as a method for man to earn God's favor, then why was it given? For an answer, let's read what the apostle Paul states about the Law in his letter to the Christians in Rome.

Now we know that whatever the law says, it says to those who are under the law, so that every mouth may be silenced and <u>the whole world held accountable to God</u>. Therefore, <u>no one will be declared righteous in God's sight by the works of the law</u>; rather, <u>through the law, we become conscious of our sin.</u> (Romans 3:19-20)

Paul states that we can never obtain righteousness – that is, salvation – by trying to obey the Law. So, contrary to popular belief, the Law was never meant to act as a ladder by which mankind could climb up to God. Rather, through the Law, we become aware of our sin. Meaning that, instead of acting as a ladder, the Law was given as a mirror so that mankind can see just how sinful we are and just how far short we fall with respect to God's holiness. And, then, once we come to realize that we are sinners and that we are accountable to God for our sin, that will hopefully cause us to simply seek out God's mercy. Because, make no mistake, God is the God of mercy. He is merciful to us today, and He was merciful to the Israelites back then. Which brings us to the third and final reason that the Law was given.

If you've been paying close attention, then you've realized that we've got a conundrum. The Bible is clear that God is just, meaning that He must punish sin. And as we saw with Adam and Eve, the just penalty of sin is death and being cast out of God's presence. When we break His commands, we then owe Him a life-debt. So, how exactly can the holy Judge of the universe have a relationship with a bunch of wretched sinners that deserve both death and separation from Him? He can't simply dismiss our sins, ignoring the penalty that is due, because then He would no longer be just. If He did so, then one might call that act 'forgiveness' or 'mercy,' but what it certainly isn't is justice. The definition of justice is 'Getting what we deserve,' while the definition of mercy is 'Not getting what we deserve.' So, how then can God be both just and merciful at the same time? It seems like a contradiction. Well, this is where the ceremonial statutes of the Law come into play.

God gave to Moses incredibly detailed and specific instructions on how to properly worship Him – for example, how to construct the tabernacle and all of the items found within; how to establish a priestly order that would act as a mediator between the people and God; and how to perform various sacrificial offerings, including the killing of certain animals and the sprinkling of their blood on God's altar. The last part – the killing of animals – may be offensive to our 21st century sensibilities, and the truth is that it was offensive. It couldn't have been pleasant to hear the cries of pain bellowing forth from the bulls and goats as their throats were cut. God was showing the Israelites that He is a holy and righteous Judge, who takes sin very seriously. He was showing them that their sin was an offensive, ugly thing to Him that had to be punished and, therefore, the means by which He would deal with their sin would also be offensive and ugly. But as ugly as the sacrificing of animals was, it was also necessary. At least, it was necessary if they wanted their sins to be forgiven. For, as I mentioned in the previous paragraph, the consequence of sin is death. A life is owed when we sin against God. Blood must be shed. The writer of the book of Hebrews states, *'For when every commandment of the law had been declared by Moses to all the people, he took the blood of calves and goats, with water and scarlet wool and hyssop, and sprinkled both the book itself and all the people, saying 'This is the blood of the covenant* *that God commanded for you.' And in the same way, he sprinkled with blood both the tent and all the vessels used in worship. Indeed, under the law almost everything is purified with blood, and <u>without the shedding of blood there is no forgiveness of sins.</u>'* (Hebrews 9:19-22)

God was teaching the Israelites what I believe is one of the most important principles in all the Bible, and it is this: God's merciful plan of salvation would involve substitution. It is a principle that is found throughout Scripture – in the saving of Abraham's son, Isaac (Genesis 22), in the saving of the Israelites in Egypt during the Passover (Exodus 12), and certainly here in the sacrificial system of the Mosaic Law. The Israelite sinner would have only two choices in dealing with the penalty of his sin. He could either choose to pay off the debt himself with his own life and by being separated from God for eternity, or he could choose to trust in God's plan, choosing instead a substitute – a bull or goat without blemish – to satisfy the life-debt. If the sinner chose the latter option, then God would consider that the guilt of his sin would be transferred from him to the animal. Through the shedding of the animal's blood and its death, that person's sin would be atoned for and the life-debt paid. The sinner would, therefore, be forgiven, at least temporarily. For the sacrificial system given through the Law could only ever act as a temporary measure. It could only ever partially fulfill God's just demand that sin be atoned for. But why is that?

As is stated in the first chapter of Genesis, humans were originally made in God's image. That fact makes us special. Nothing else in all of God's creation possesses the inherent value that we have. Therefore, the life of a bull or a goat – even one without blemish – could never truly be a sufficient substitute on our behalf, because they do not possess the same value as humans. Using a current day example, if I borrow your car and demolish it in a wreck, then I would owe you a car-debt. And you would expect that the vehicle I replace yours with would be of equal worth. You certainly would not accept me giving you a bicycle in the place of your car. Similarly, only the sacrificial death of a being of equal or greater value to mankind could ever truly act as a worthy replacement for the life-debt that the sinner owes. But who or what could possibly be that substitute? In all of God's creation, only a human being has enough value to serve as an adequate substitute for another human being. However, the Bible is clear that all men are sinful by nature. Which means that the death of one ordinary man could never pay off the sins of another, because his death would only be sufficient enough to pay off his own life-debt. He could never pay off the penalty of his sins and those of another human being, as well. So, we've got ourselves another conundrum, don't we? Unless we want to pay the penalty of our sins ourselves, then we must have a substitute that (1.) possesses, at the least, the same value of humanity's worth but (2.) is also without sin. But from where exactly is this substitute going to come? Well, fortunately for us, the LORD is all-wise. Therefore, His plan of salvation would solve this seemingly impossible situation, and we will explore His solution in future chapters.

In summary of this section, we can see that God gave His Law for three reasons: He gave it out of love, for the good of His people, to protect them from harm and to help them flourish; He gave it to display to the world both the heights of His holiness and justice and also the depths of the depravity of the sinful human heart; and He gave it to teach His people that salvation – the forgiveness of sins – would come through a substitute's blood and death.

So, with the giving of the Law and with God's people on the verge of entering the Promised Land, we can see that God's kingdom is about to be fulfilled. And if we skip forward one book, to the book of Joshua, we can read of the Israelite nation finally entering and settling in the land of Canaan. Therefore, you may be thinking, "Great. That means the story is over, right? You stated that God's plan of salvation would be fulfilled when His kingdom was finally established. And it's now established. So, why are there sixty more books in the Bible to read?"

To answer that question, I need to remind you of a topic I introduced in the last chapter – the difference between God's partial kingdom versus His final, perfect kingdom. The Israelites entering into Canaan only partially fulfilled God's kingdom requirements, and the reason is because the issues of sin and death still had not been solved in a complete and ultimate manner. As I already mentioned, the Old Testament sacrificial system was only a temporary measure in dealing with sin. What's more, the Israelites, while being God's people, were not truly under His rule, for they did not willingly and joyfully submit to His authority. They certainly didn't love Him with all their heart, soul, and might. Remember what God had spoken to Moses right before he died, *'Then this people will rise and whore after the foreign gods among them in the land that they are entering, and they will forsake me and break my covenant that I have made with them.'* (Deuteronomy 31:16) And why were they going to rebel against God? We've already looked at the answer to that question, as well. *'But to this day, the LORD has not given you a heart to understand or eyes to see or ears to hear.'* (Deuteronomy 29:2) The Israelites' problem was a heart issue. Due to their sinful natures, the Israelites were going to forsake God and begin to worship false gods. That does not sound like being 'under God's rule, enjoying God's blessing.' If God's people were ever going to be able to willingly and lovingly submit to His authority, then God Himself was going to have to eradicate the sinful heart found within mankind. For there is no doubt that we humans are not capable of doing so. And, not surprisingly, God promised His people that He would accomplish that very thing.

'And the LORD your God will <u>circumcise your heart</u> and the heart of your offspring, so that you will love the LORD your God with all your heart and with all your soul, that you may live.' (Deuteronomy 30:6)

The Israelites probably had absolutely no idea what a 'circumcision of the heart' would entail. Perhaps, you don't either. It's likely that they wondered, "How is that even possible? Is God literally going to cut away pieces of our hearts?" Well, those are great questions, and to discover the answers, you will need to read on.

Chapter 6: God Promises an Eternal King (2nd Samuel 7)

Throughout the Scriptures, we can read of God making numerous promises. Usually, the promises were given through a prophet to God's people but, at times, He spoke to those who were not part of His chosen people at all. Regardless of the recipient, though, His promises were always incredibly profound and, typically, mysterious and veiled, as well. Occasionally, they seemed outright impossible. To start, I'd like to remind you of a few of God's promises that we have already looked at in this study.

In the Garden of Eden, God declared to the serpent – the devil – these words, *'And I will put enmity between you and the woman, and between your offspring and hers; he will crush your head and you will strike his heel.'* (Genesis 3:15)

Adam and Eve – and even the devil, himself – must have thought, "Who exactly will this 'serpent-crusher' be?"

Thousands of years later, we read of God making this promise:

Now the LORD said to Abram, 'Go from your country and your people and your father's household to the land that I will show you. And I will make you into a great nation, and I will bless you; I will make your name great, so that you will be a blessing. I will bless those who bless you, and whoever curses you I will curse; and all the peoples on earth will be blessed through you.' (Genesis 12:1-3)

We already saw God partially fulfill this promise, specifically the 'impossible' portion of it – that is, turning Abraham into a great nation by granting him and his barren wife a child. But even afterwards, Abraham and Sarah must have wondered how God was going to bless all the peoples of the earth through them.

God also promised Abraham, *'To your offspring I will give this land.'* (Genesis 12:7)

It took several hundred years, but in the previous chapter, we saw God, in His perfect timing, finally bringing the Israelites – Abraham's descendants – to the Promised Land. But before they entered Canaan, God – through His prophet Moses – swore this to them:

'And <u>the LORD your God will circumcise your heart</u> and the heart of your offspring, so that you will love the LORD your God with all your heart and with all your soul, that you may live.' (Deuteronomy 30:6)

I feel confident in stating that the people of God did not understand the meaning of that promise at all – neither the process by which it would be fulfilled nor its profound ramifications.

In this chapter, we will examine another of God's significant promises, but before we get to that promise, I feel some background is necessary. In the book of Joshua, we can read of the Israelites – with God's mighty assistance – entering and conquering the Promised Land. Despite them not perfectly obeying God and His commands during this time, overall, the settlement of Canaan went well.

So, the LORD gave Israel all the land He had sworn to give their ancestors, and they took possession of it and settled there. The LORD gave them rest on every side, just as He has sworn to their ancestors. Not one of their enemies withstood them; the LORD gave all their enemies into their hands. Not one of all the LORD's good promises to Israel failed; every one was fulfilled. (Joshua 22:43-45)

That actually sounds fantastic, doesn't it? However, let's not forget the condemning words that God had previously spoken to Moses before his death.

And the LORD said to Moses, 'Behold, you are about to lie down with your fathers. Then this people will rise and whore after the foreign gods among them in the land that they are entering, and they will forsake me and break my covenant that I have made with them.' (Deuteronomy 31:16)

Therefore, it should surprise no one that, generally speaking, things went poorly for the Israelites after they settled in Canaan, particularly after their leader, Joshua, died. In fact, in the book of Judges, we can read of a sad, never-ending cycle taking place over the course of several hundred years. Instead of summarizing the events myself, I'll simply let God's Word speak for itself:

After that whole generation had been gathered to their ancestors, another generation grew up who neither knew the LORD nor what He had done for Israel. Then the Israelites did evil in the eyes of the LORD and served the Baals. They forsook the LORD, the God of their ancestors, who had brought them out of Egypt. They followed and worshipped various gods of the people around them. They aroused the LORD's anger because they forsook Him and served Baal and the Ashtoreths. In His anger against Israel, the LORD gave them into the hands of raiders who plundered them. He sold them into the hands of their enemies all around, whom they were no longer able to resist. Whenever Israel went out to fight, the hand of the LORD was against them to defeat them, just as He had sworn to them. They were in great distress.

Then the LORD raised up judges who saved them out of the hands of these raiders. Yet they would not listen to their judges and prostituted themselves to other gods and worshipped them. They quickly turned from the ways of their ancestors, who had been obedient to the LORD's commands. Whenever the LORD raised up a judge for them, He was with the judge and saved them out of the hands of their enemies as long as the judge lived; for the LORD relented because of their groaning under those who oppressed and afflicted them. But when the judge died, the people returned to ways even more corrupt than those of their ancestors, following other gods and serving and worshipping them. They refused to give up their evil practices and stubborn ways. (Judges 2:10-19)

There is a proverb which states, *'As a dog returns to its vomit, so a fool repeats his folly.'* (Proverbs 26:11). The Israelites were the living embodiment of this truth. They had made an absolute mess of themselves and the Promised Land, causing a downward spiral of chaos and apostasy. In fact, the description above sounds about as far from God's kingdom as one can get. They certainly were not God's people, in God's place, under God's rule, enjoying God's blessing. The last verse of the book of Judges declares this:

In those days, Israel had no king; everyone did as they saw fit. (Judges 21:25)

Sounds very contemporary, doesn't it? With no one doing what God states is right and pure but, rather, doing what they see fit. Doing whatever it is that pleases them. And people wonder why the world is the way it is.

Well, after several hundred years of being stuck in this cycle, repeatedly being defeated and oppressed by their enemies, the Israelites finally decided, "You know what? Our current circumstances are not pleasing to us. We need to do something different." Which actually sounds promising, right? As if, maybe, they were finally starting to wise up. When I worked as a counselor, I routinely told my students and occasionally even some parents, "If what you're currently doing isn't working for you, then try something different. Perhaps, this new course of action won't be the solution either, but we know for sure that what you're doing now is not achieving the results that you desire." Unfortunately, we should not congratulate the Israelites too quickly on their decision. The truly wise choice would have been for them to repent of their apostasy and turn back to their Redeemer and their Source of Strength. Instead, this is what they decided:

So, all the elders of Israel gathered together and came to Samuel [who was Israel's last God-fearing judge] *at Ramah. They said to him, 'You are old and your sons do not follow your ways; now appoint a king to lead us, <u>such as all the other nations have</u>.'* (1 Samuel 8:4-5)

God had called His people to be holy – that is, different than the rest of the world. And here they are, deciding that they want to be just like all the other nations around them. Being like the rest of the world – and specifically worshipping the world's gods – was what got them into their current predicament in the first place. So, if you've never read or heard of this part of the story and, therefore, don't know what happens next, then you'd probably think that God would reject their request. For the nation of Israel was supposed to be a theocracy, with God as their leader, right? Instead, here is how He answered:

And the LORD said to Samuel, 'Obey the voice of the people in all that they say to you, for they have not rejected you, but they have rejected me from being king over them. According to all the deeds that they have done, from the day I brought them up out of Egypt even to this day, forsaking me and serving other gods, so they are also doing to you. Now then, obey their voice, only you shall solemnly warn them and show them the ways of the king who shall reign over them.' (1 Samuel 8:7-9)

So, Samuel proceeded to warn the Israelites of what would happen if they lived under a human monarch. This king would take their sons and daughters, their crops and animals, their servants and their money. Samuel warned them that they would ultimately be the king's slaves. Of course, the Israelites refused to heed the warnings, basically crying out, "We don't care! We want to be like everyone else so give us a king!" It is almost comical how poorly the Israelites are portrayed in the Scriptures. At least, it would be funny if it wasn't so sad and convicting. They come off looking like spoiled, rebellious, bratty little children. Despite their behavior, though, God, through Samuel, gave them what they wanted and appointed a king to rule over them. You won't be shocked to discover that this first king's reign did not go well, and the reason is because this king, Saul, did not ultimately listen to and obey God's instructions.

Before we continue, it is important to note that the Israelites' desire for a king had not surprised God in the least. In fact, back in Deuteronomy 17, before the people had even entered the Promised Land, God had given several commands regarding how this future king of Israel should live. Among other things, God stated that he was not to abuse his position for personal gain, giving specific warnings against him acquiring numerous wives and abundant wealth. This king was to be a humble servant of God, who faithfully obeyed all of God's commands, even going so far as to copying down the entire Law of God and keeping that personal scroll with him at all times so that he could study and meditate on it. Well, Saul did not fulfill those commands, so the LORD set His heart on another, a shepherd boy named David who was from the line of Judah.

To discover why that is important, we need to go back several centuries to a time when the Israelites were still living in Egypt but were not yet slaves. Right before Abraham's grandson Jacob died, he gathered all of his sons around him to give them a final blessing. Here is what he said to his fourth son, Judah:

'Judah, your brothers will praise you; your hand will be on the neck of your enemies; your father's sons will bow down to you. You are a lion's cub, Judah; you return from the prey, my son. Like a lion, he crouches and lies down, like a lioness – who dares to rouse him? The scepter will not depart from Judah, nor the ruler's staff from between his feet, until he to whom it belongs shall come and the obedience of the nations shall be his.' (Genesis 49:8-10)

This blessing from Jacob to Judah was also clearly a prophetic message from God. A scepter belongs in the hands of a monarch. So, God was foretelling of a future king who would come from the line of Judah; a king who would rule all the nations, which brings us to King David and, finally, to our main chapter, 2nd Samuel 7.

Up to this point in the story, David – who, by no coincidence, was a descendent of Judah – had been an amazing king. As a young man, God had blessed David by placing His Spirit upon him (1st Samuel 16:13), and as a consequence, he became a powerful warrior. Later, as king, with God's mighty hand remaining on him, he became Israel's greatest military commander, defeating all of the kingdom's enemies.

The first verse of 2nd Samuel 7 states, *'After the king was settled in his palace and the LORD had given him rest from all his enemies around...'*

For centuries, due to the apostasy of God's people, the Promised Land had been in chaos and turmoil. War was constant. But now, finally, there was rest in the kingdom.

But David's admirable characteristics didn't consist solely of his military prowess. More importantly, he was a man who loved God deeply. He possessed a poet's heart and wrote about half of the book of Psalms, many of which are songs of praise and worship. We can see his desire to honor God in the next verse:

...he [David] said to Nathan the prophet, 'Here I am, living in a house of cedar, while the ark of God remains in a tent.' (2 Samuel 7:2)

In essence, David was saying, "God is worthy of ultimate praise and glory, so why is He dwelling in a tent when I'm living in a palace? That's not right." So, David was planning on building a temple for God. A magnificent house in which the ark could permanently reside. A dwelling that would display the majesty of the LORD. But God had other plans.

But that night, the word of the LORD came to Nathan, saying: 'Go and tell my servant David, "This is what the LORD says: Are you the one to build me a house to dwell in? I have not dwelt in a house from the day I brought the Israelites up out of Egypt to this day. I have been moving from place to place with a tent as my dwelling. Wherever I have moved with all the Israelites, did I ever say to any of their rulers whom I commanded to shepherd my people Israel, 'Why have you not built me a house of cedar?'" Now then, tell my servant David, 'This is what the LORD Almighty says: <u>I took you from the pasture, from tending the flock, and appointed you prince over my people Israel</u>. I have been with you wherever you have gone, and I have cut off all your enemies from before you. Now <u>I will make your name great</u>, like the names of the greatest men on earth. And <u>I will provide a place for my people Israel</u> and will plant them so that they can have a home of their own and no longer be disturbed. Wicked people will not oppress them anymore, as they did at the beginning and have done ever since the time I appointed *judges over my people Israel. I will also give you rest from all your enemies.'* (2 Samuel 7:5-11a)

Reading through these verses again, I was struck by how similar God's actions towards David were to His actions with Abraham. Centuries before, the LORD had called Abraham out of a place where he felt safe and comfortable – Haran – and placed him into a position of leadership over God's people, with Abraham becoming the 'father' of the entire future nation of Israel. Additionally, He promised Abraham that he would give His people a land of their own. And, now, here, we read of God taking David out of a place where he felt safe and comfortable – in the pasture tending to the flocks – and placing him into a position of leadership over God's people, with David becoming – in God's words – the 'prince' of the Israelites. Likewise, God also promised David, *'...I will provide a place for my people Israel...'* And finally, notice that God promised both men that He would make their names great. It's as if God's words and actions toward both men are part of the same overarching promise and plan.

But God continues speaking to David, and here is where the promise turns unique.

'The LORD declares to you that the LORD himself will establish a house for you: When your days are over and you rest with your ancestors, I will raise up your offspring to succeed you, your own flesh and blood, and I will establish his kingdom. He is the one who will build a house for my Name, and I will establish the throne of his kingdom forever. I will be his father, and he will be my son. When he does wrong, I will punish him with a rod wielded by men, with floggings inflicted by human hands. But my love will never be taken away from him, as I took it away from Saul, who I removed from before you. Your house and your kingdom will endure forever before me; your throne will be established forever.' (2 Samuel 7:11b-16)

On first reading, this pronouncement by God may not seem to be so profound, but it is. And to explain exactly why, I need to first discuss the difficulty of interpreting prophecy. As I mentioned at the beginning of this chapter, God's promises can, at times, be mysterious and veiled, and one reason is because they can have multiple meanings. Charles Swindoll once likened interpreting prophecy to trying to find the highest peak while walking in a mountain range. You look upward, and from where you're standing, you see what you believe to be the summit. So, you start walking towards it, but when you reach the top, you realize that there is actually another mountain on the other side that is taller but that had been previously hidden from view. Similarly, prophecy can possess both near and far-reaching ramifications, and it's not until we have already gone past the near 'peak' that we can finally see the other one off in the distance. Therefore, on the surface, this promise from God to David seemingly is simply referring to David's son, Solomon. For, if we read on in the book of 1st Kings, we can see that, out of all of David's offspring, Solomon was the one who ruled after David died and who built a great temple for the LORD.

However, in this promise from God to David, there is a word that is used that makes it clear that God can't be referring exclusively to Solomon. That word is 'forever.'

'He is the one who will build a house for my Name, and I will establish the throne of his kingdom forever.'

Well, not only did Solomon, himself, not live forever, but neither did the royal reign of his descendants. In the next chapter, we will explore in a bit more detail exactly what happened to both the kingdom of Israel and to David's line, but I'll go ahead and spoil the story for you by telling you that neither of them last. At least, not in a traditional way of thinking. But how can that be? God just made this promise to David:

'Your house and your kingdom will endure forever before me; your throne will be established forever.'

Since God always fulfills His promises, then He must be referring to someone other than Solomon in this promise. Additionally, He must be referring to some other type of kingdom and throne. Regardless of what exactly God means here, there is no doubt that this mentioning of eternity makes this promise different than all the other promises that we've looked at so far, and that is what makes it so profound. For thousands of years, God had been making promises to His people, but now, we are seeing that there is an eternal aspect to this one. When David said that he wanted to build a house for God, the LORD replied, "No. Instead, I'm going to build you a house." Meaning an eternal, royal dynasty.

Now, I highly doubt that David fully and truly understood what God meant by this promise or how exactly the LORD was going to fulfill it – which we will discover in future chapters. Nevertheless, David clearly saw it as a blessing, for the entire second half of the chapter consists of David's prayer of praise to the LORD. It's a wonderful outpouring of humility, gratitude, and faith, and I encourage you to read it on your own.

Before we conclude, I would like to bring up a principle that can be found in the Scripture above. It's a principle that is repeated throughout the Bible and, therefore, I think it is quite important. Earlier, we read of the Israelites sinning by asking for Samuel to place a king over them. I am confident in saying that they sinned by making this request because God made it clear that the motivation behind their request was wrong. God specifically told Samuel that, in asking for a king, they were rejecting Him. They were not asking for a king who would be *subservient* to the LORD and would, therefore, lead them in God's ways. On the contrary, they were asking for a king to *replace* the LORD, and that – rejecting God – is the ultimate sin. However, as I already mentioned, God knew that they were going to make this sinful request as seen in both His prior instructions to Moses regarding how Israelite kings should comport themselves and also through the prophecy that Jacob had made about the scepter not departing the house of Judah. Then, decades after the Israelites' sinful request, God would make an incredibly significant promise to King David, a promise that would tie into His plan of salvation and have eternal ramifications for the entire world. The point I'm trying to make is that God is so powerful and so wise that He is able to weave even the sinful acts of rebellious, disobedient men into the tapestry of His overarching, sovereign plans. Absolutely nothing surprises the LORD, and nothing is too difficult for the LORD. How amazing He is.

Therefore, I would like to end by encouraging you. If you have made such a mess of your life that you don't think God could ever use you in His plans, I promise you that He can. In fact, I am confident in saying that He loves doing that very thing – taking broken, sinful people; redeeming them out of their brokenness and their slavery to sin; and then using them for His kingdom and His glory. He did it for the apostle Paul (see Acts 9). He did it for me. And I know He can do it for you, as well. You simply need to ask Him.

Chapter 7: The Messiah Will Be a Suffering Servant (Isaiah 53)

At the end of the previous chapter, we saw God – through the prophet Nathan – making a promise to King David that He would establish David's kingdom forever. That promise was different than all the other of God's promises that we'd examined up to that point due to it containing the element of eternity.

'Your house and your kingdom will endure forever before me; your throne will be established forever.' (2 Samuel 7:16)

With that promise in mind, you would think that Israel – with David's descendants sitting on the throne – would remain as a powerful and influential kingdom until the end of time, much less for the next few generations to come. However, nothing could be further from the truth. While Israel did prosper during the reign of Solomon, David's son, serious trouble began during the end of his life. In his old age, Solomon was enticed away from the LORD by the gods of his many foreign wives. He even went so far as to build temples to these false gods, drawing the ire of God.

The LORD became angry with Solomon because his heart had turned away from the LORD, the God of Israel, who had appeared to him twice. Although he had forbidden Solomon to follow other gods, Solomon did not keep the LORD's commands. So, the LORD said to Solomon, 'Since this is your attitude and you have not kept my covenant and my decrees, which I commanded you, I will most certainly tear the kingdom away from you and give it to one of your subordinates. Nevertheless, for the sake of David your father, I will not do it during your lifetime. I will tear it out of the hand of your son.' (1 Kings 11:9-12)

Sure enough, a rebellion broke out within the land, and once Solomon's son took the throne, a civil war ensued with the kingdom splitting in two. Ten of the twelve tribes of Israel formed together in the north and became known as 'Israel' while the other two tribes were located in the southern part of the land and were known as

'Judah.' And while there were a few exceptions, as a whole, the monarchs of both kingdoms were not God-fearing in the least. They worshipped false gods, even those requiring child sacrifices. In fact, if you read through the books of 1st and 2nd Kings, almost every king is described with these words, "He did evil in the eyes of the LORD." That phrase is repeated over and over.

Not surprisingly, the people in both kingdoms followed their respective kings' lead and fell under God's just wrath. Over the course of several centuries, the people rejected God and His rule. Therefore, God removed His blessings from them, and, eventually, He even removed them from the land that He had once promised to their ancestors. In 722 B.C., the LORD, as judgment upon His people, sent the Assyrians to wipe out the northern kingdom of Israel and take its inhabitants into exile. Unfortunately, the people in Judah did not learn from the lesson that God had sent their northern kin, and in 586 B.C., they too were conquered, this time by the Babylonians. The invaders even went so far as to completely destroy the magnificent temple that Solomon had built for the LORD, but only after plundering it of its contents. The last chapter of 2nd Kings states this, *'So Judah went into captivity, away from her land.'* (2 Kings 25:21b) What had once been a great and powerful kingdom was now in shambles with its people exiled. Not since their four-hundred years of slavery in Egypt had the Israelites been is such a sorry state. They were about as far from being God's people, in God's place, under God's rule, enjoying God's blessing as one could get.

But I want to make it clear that, while God's judgment upon His people for their apostasy was devastating, it was not immediate. As we have seen, the LORD is a patient and merciful God. Therefore, during the centuries of the Israelites' rebellion against Him, God had not been silent. He had repeatedly spoken to His people through various prophets. Starting with the book of Isaiah, there are seventeen different prophetic books in the Old Testament which tell us of God's message through these prophets. Some of the prophets were based in the northern kingdom of Israel. Some were located in the southern kingdom of Judah, while others had lived in exile. Also, not all of the prophets lived during the exact same time period.

However, as a whole, regardless of their differing locations and time frames, almost all of the prophets had the same basic message from the LORD, a message in two parts. First, they spoke a message of warning that God's judgment was coming due to the people's apostasy. And, secondly, they spoke a message of hope – a promise that God would rescue a remnant of His people out of that judgment. Additionally, some of the prophets indicated that God's rescue would come through a special leader and even referenced the promise that God had made centuries before to King David. What follows are a few examples of this prophetic message:

For to us a child is born, to us a son is given, and the government will be on his shoulders. And he will be called Wonderful Counselor, Mighty God, Everlasting Father, Prince of Peace. Of the greatness of his government and peace there will be no end. He will reign on David's throne and over his kingdom, establishing and upholding it with justice and righteousness from that time on and forever. The zeal of the LORD Almighty will accomplish this. (Isaiah 9:6-7)

'The days are coming,' declares the LORD, 'when I will raise up for David a righteous Branch, a King who will reign wisely and do what is just and right in the land. In his days Judah will be saved and Israel will live in safety. This is the name by which he will be called: The LORD Our Righteous Savior.' (Jeremiah 23:5-6)

'My servant David will be king over them, and they will all have one shepherd. They will follow my laws and be careful to keep my decrees. They will live in the land I gave to my servant Jacob, the land where your ancestors lived. They and their children and their children's children will live there forever, and David my servant will be their prince forever. I will make a covenant of peace with them; it will be an everlasting covenant. I will establish them and increase their numbers, and I will put my sanctuary among them forever. My dwelling place will be with them; I will be their God, and they will be my people, Then, the nations will know that I the LORD make Israel holy, when my sanctuary is among them forever.' (Ezekiel 37:24-28)

In my vision at night, I looked and there before me was one like a son of man, coming with the clouds of heaven. He approached the Ancient of Days and was led into his presence. He was given authority, glory and sovereign power; all nations and people of every language worshipped him. His dominion is an everlasting dominion that will not pass away, and his kingdom is one that will never be destroyed. (Daniel 7:13-14)

'But you, Bethlehem Ephrathah, though you are small among the clans of Judah, out of you will come for me one who will be ruler over Israel, whose origins are from old, from ancient times. Therefore, Israel will be abandoned until the time when she who is in labor bears a son, and the rest of his brothers return to join the Israelites. He will stand and shepherd his flock in the strength of the LORD, in the majesty of the name of the LORD his God. And they will live securely, for then his greatness will reach the ends of the earth.' (Micah 5:2-4)

In these prophecies, we can see a recurring theme. This special, chosen one of God – from the line of David – would bring about salvation for God's people. He would rule with justice, wisdom and righteousness, and His reign would last forever.

Of course, the Israelites – exiled to a foreign country – eagerly anticipated the arrival of this chosen one, for they longed for the restoration of their nation. Decades later, they were allowed to repatriate their land and rebuild both the city of Jerusalem and the temple, but, even still, their kingdom was never the same. During the centuries that followed, the Israelites were usually under the control of foreign powers – be it the Persians, the Greeks and, around the turn of the millennium, the Romans. The Israelite kingdom never again reached the heights of power and influence experienced during King David's reign. Therefore, generation after generation searched desperately for this promised king who would finally lead Israel back to its former glory.

I think it's important to mention that, though it is not specifically stated in the Old Testament Scriptures, the Israelites had a title for this future ruler – the Messiah. It is a Hebrew word that means 'the anointed one.' In the Greek, it is translated as 'Christ.' To fully understand the significance of the title, we need to go back to the book of 1st Samuel, to when David was still a shepherd boy tending to his father's flock in the hills. After Israel's first king, Saul, had shown himself unworthy of the position, the LORD told Samuel that He had chosen a new king. When Samuel finally met David, God gave him these instructions, *'Then, the LORD said 'Rise and anoint him; this is the one.' So, Samuel took the horn of oil and anointed him in the presence of his brothers, and from that day on the Spirit of the LORD came powerfully upon David.'* (1 Samuel 16:12-13). The anointing of oil signified that God had chosen the individual for a special role and purpose – in David's case, to be king. And since David had been an incredible warrior and military commander, the Israelites expected that this promised Messiah would be the same.

However, as we have seen throughout this study, God's ways are not our ways. He seems to love turning our plans and expectations upside down, which brings us finally to our passage for this chapter (Isaiah 53), and to what is, I believe, one of the most significant prophecies in all of Scripture.

God spoke to His people through the prophet, Isaiah, and told them that, though they had been recipients of His judgment due to their rebellion against Him, it would not last. The LORD promised that He would lead them into salvation, and, then, Isaiah transitions into these verses.

'See, my servant will act wisely; he will be raised and lifted up and highly exalted.' (Isaiah 52:13)

Suddenly, seemingly out of nowhere, God goes from talking about how He will save His people to talking about this unnamed servant.

'Just as there were many who were appalled at him – his appearance was so disfigured beyond that of any human being and his form marred beyond human likeness – so he will sprinkle many nations, and kings will shut their mouths because of him. For what they were not told, they will see, and what they have not heard, they

will understand. Who has believed our message and to whom has the arm of the LORD been revealed?' (Isaiah 52:14-53:1)

I warned before that prophecy can be confusing, and this certainly must have been to the people who were hearing it for the first time. In verse thirteen, God – through His prophet – was speaking about His servant in the future tense, and then suddenly, He combines both past and future tenses in the next two sentences. This combination of past and future tense will be seen throughout the rest of the passage. But what shouldn't be missed here is that this future servant would clearly not be attractive in the traditional sense. People would be appalled at his disfigured and marred appearance. And what in the world could 'sprinkle the nations' possibly mean? The Old Testament temple priests sprinkled the altar of God with the blood of the sacrificial bulls and goats, but was that related at all to this sprinkling of the nations? Make no mistake, though, this unnamed servant would reveal to the world a message that had never before been understood.

'He grew up before him like a tender shoot, and like a root out of dry ground. He had no beauty or majesty to attract us to him, nothing in his appearance that we should desire him. He was despised and rejected by mankind, a man of suffering and familiar with pain. Like one from whom people hide their faces, he was despised, and we held him in low esteem.' (Isaiah 53:2-3)

Whoever this servant is, he cannot possibly be the Messiah, right? The Israelites believed the Messiah would be a powerful, military leader. One who would lead the people to victory over their oppressors and restore the kingdom to its former glory. That idea does not square at all with the above description of this lowly, despised, suffering servant. But wait – the upcoming verses would become even more confusing to the Israelite readers.

'Surely, he took up our pain and bore our suffering, yet we considered him punished by God, stricken by him and afflicted. But he was pierced for our transgressions, he was crushed for our iniquities; the punishment that brought us peace was on him, and by his wounds, we are healed. We all, like sheep, have gone astray;

each of us has turned to our own way; and the LORD has laid on him the iniquity of us all.' (Isaiah 53:4-6)

This does not sound like a conquering hero at all. The Messiah is supposed to be a victorious leader – not punished, stricken, afflicted, pierced, and crushed. Additionally, Isaiah is clear that the punishment this servant would receive would not be due to his own wrongdoing. He would be punished on behalf of the people. More so, while this punishment would be brutal for the servant, it would actually bring about peace and healing for others. My hope is that this description should sound familiar to you. I stated in chapter five that one of the most important principles that God was teaching His people by giving them the Law – specifically, the sacrificial system found in the ceremonial portion of the Law – was that His salvation would come through substitution. That the forgiveness of sin would come through a substitute's death and blood. If that thought hadn't come to you before, then the next verse most certainly would have brought it to mind.

'He was oppressed and afflicted, yet he did not open his mouth; he was led <u>like a lamb to the slaughter</u>, and <u>as a sheep</u> before its shearers is silent, so he did not open his mouth.' (Isaiah 53:7)

In the sacrificial system, a sinner would bring a bull or goat without blemish to the temple priests, who would kill it in order to atone for the sins of that person. Likewise, this servant is described as a lamb being led to the slaughter.

'By oppression and judgment, he was taken away. Yet who of his generation protested? For he was <u>cut off from the land of the living</u>; for the transgressions of my people, he was punished. He was <u>assigned a grave</u> with the wicked and with the rich <u>in his death</u>, though he had done <u>no violence, nor was any deceit</u> in his mouth.' (Isaiah 53:8-9)

These verses make two things clear: first, this servant would be more than just punished. He would actually die – cut off from the land of the living, assigned to a grave. Secondly, the prophet reiterates that this servant's punishment and death would not be due to his own sin, for he was without violence and deceit.

'Yet it was the LORD's will to crush him and cause him to suffer...' (Isaiah 53:10a)

The punishment and death that this servant would suffer would not be accidental. It would be part of God's sovereign plan. God, Himself, would ordain for this to happen.

'...and though, the LORD makes his life an offering for sin, he will see his offspring and prolong his days, and the will of the LORD will prosper in his hand. After he has suffered, he will see the light of life and be satisfied; by his knowledge my righteous servant will justify many, and he will bear their iniquities.' (Isaiah 53:10b-11)

The punishment and death of this righteous servant would not be the end of the story. The LORD God would be pleased with his sacrifice, and he would see the light of life.

'Therefore, I will give him a portion among the great, and he will divide the spoils with the strong, because he poured out his life unto death, and was numbered with the transgressors. For he bore the sin of many, and made intercession for the transgressors.' (Isaiah 53:12)

Though this righteous servant was not a transgressor himself, he would be counted as one in order to act as a mediator between them and the holy Judge of the universe. And because of this selfless sacrifice, he would be honored – by receiving a portion among the great and the spoils of the strong.

So, in conclusion, would this unknown and unnamed, suffering servant predicted here in the prophecy of Isaiah be the same as the kingly Messiah promised in those other prophecies that we've already read? I can guarantee you that the Israelites of that time did not think so. I am confident in saying that even Isaiah didn't truly and fully understand the meaning of his prophecy. And, if you are new to the Bible, then perhaps you don't either, but that will all start to change in the next chapter. Up until now, I have been taking you through many mysterious and confusing promises and prophecies, but in chapter eight, we will finally begin exploring the answers.

Chapter 8: The Messiah Arrives (Luke 1-2)

Alistair Begg once stated, "To be a complete Christian, you need the complete Bible." Meaning that, in order for me to fully understand the single, overarching story found in God's Word, I can't dismiss the Old Testament as being irrelevant to Christianity and only applicable to the Jews. He has routinely likened the Scriptures to a two-act play, and I would clarify his analogy further by saying that the Bible is similar to, specifically, a two-act play of a mystery. If a person arrives late to the play – after the intermission – then he won't understand anything that is happening in the second act. He'll be constantly disturbing the person sitting next to him, asking such questions as, "Who is that? What does that mean? What are they referencing?" For, in the first act, the groundwork is laid. Countless clues are given through promises and prophecies. My hope is that I adequately laid that groundwork for you in the previous chapters.

Conversely, if a person left the play at the end of the first act, then they would never discover the answer to the mystery. They'd never know how all of the promises and prophecies were fulfilled. And that is the predicament in which our Jewish friends find themselves today – knowing well the details of the Law, the Prophets, and the Psalms, and still longing for the arrival of their promised Messiah. But in this chapter, I will show that God has already sent His Chosen One, and I will do so by focusing on chapters one and two of the Gospel according to Luke. Incidentally, the word 'gospel' is derived from an old Anglo-Saxon word and simply means 'good news.' However, before I begin exploring the good news of how God fulfilled His promises, I think a little background is necessary.

About four hundred years passed from the end of Malachi – the last book of the Old Testament – to the beginning of the events described in the Gospels. And during this 'intertestamental' period, God was silent. Or, at least, according to the Bible, He was. There is no record that He spoke to any more prophets. He gave no more promises or revelations. When we pick the story up in Luke 1, the nation of Israel does have a so-called monarch on the throne, but he is not from the Davidic line, nor is he a sovereign leader. He had not been anointed king by God, but rather he'd been appointed the position by a foreign government. Like much of the world at that time, Israel was occupied by the Romans, who ruled with an iron fist. And being under the control of a bunch of pagan Gentile 'dogs' seriously chafed the Jews. They longed for God to send the Messiah – a mighty, military king – who would defeat the Romans and restore the nation of Israel to its former glory. They could have never anticipated how the LORD was going to actually answer their prayers.

In the sixth month of Elizabeth's pregnancy, God sent the angel Gabriel to Nazareth, a town in Galilee, to a virgin pledged to be married to a man named Joseph, a descendent of David. The virgin's name was Mary. The angel went to her and said, 'Greetings, you who are highly favored. The Lord is with you.' (Luke 1:26-28)

After four centuries of silence, God once again speaks, but not to King Herod sitting on the throne. Not to one of the Sadducees or Pharisees – the religious leaders of the day. Not to some skilled warrior with thousands of soldiers beneath him. Instead, He speaks to a Jewish girl living in a tiny village a hundred miles north of Jerusalem.

Mary was greatly troubled at his words and wondered what kind of greeting this might be. But the angel said to her, 'Do not be afraid, Mary; you have found favor with God. You will conceive and give birth to a son, and you are to call him Jesus. He will be great and will be called the Son of the Most High. The Lord God will give him the throne of his father David, and he will reign over Jacob's descendants forever; his kingdom will never end.' (Luke 1:29-33)

Can you imagine what must have been going through this young girl's mind upon hearing that proclamation? She had to have been overwhelmed. Not only would she miraculously get pregnant – despite being a virgin – but more than that, her son would be the promised Messiah who would sit on David's throne and whose kingly reign would last forever. Even the name that she was told to give her son would tie into the prophetic promises. Jesus is the

Greek form of Joshua, which is a derivative of Yeshua, meaning 'The LORD saves.'

'How can this be,' Mary asked the angel, 'since I am a virgin?' The angel answered, 'The Holy Spirit will come on you, and the power of the Most High will overshadow you. So, the child to be born will be called holy – the Son of God.' (Luke 1:34-35)

I'm going to pause on these two verses for a bit, for there is highly significant information found within them. In the angel's answer, we can see the trinitarian characteristic of God. The word 'trinity' is never used in the Scriptures. However, theologians coined the word to describe His mysterious three-in-one aspect. In a way that I can't truly comprehend – much less explain – the Bible is clear that there is only one God but that He consists of three distinct 'persons.' Each Person is fully God – co-equal and co-eternal – but each also has unique roles to play. I have heard numerous analogies used in an attempt to describe the Trinity – a musical chord composed of three separate notes; a cluster of three grapes; a single, family-unit consisting of a father, mother, and son – but they all fall short, for nothing of this world can truly compare to this triune dimension of God. But, regardless of whether or not we can truly comprehend the Trinity, we can see all three Persons referenced in Gabriel's words to Mary: God, the Father, is described as the Most High; the second person of the Trinity is God's Son – Jesus; and the third member is the Holy Spirit. I'm not going to delve deeper in discussing the Trinity, for that's not the purpose of this study, but I felt the need to at least mention it here for two reasons. First, because I think that it is an incredibly important doctrine for all believers to understand. And, secondly, because it ties into another doctrine, which I believe is vital in order to truly comprehend God's plan of salvation, and that doctrine is the dual natures of Jesus.

God's Word is clear that Jesus is fully man, having been born from a woman. However, the Scriptures are also clear that He is also fully God – the second member of the Trinity. He may have voluntarily relinquished some of His divine privileges in becoming human, but He was still fully God. And because He is God and because of His miraculous conception, He was not born with a sinful nature like the rest of humanity. The Bible is also clear that, throughout the rest of His life, though He was tempted, He would remain sinless. The writer of the book of Hebrews states, *'For we do not have a high priest* [Jesus] *who is unable to empathize with our weaknesses, but we have one who has been tempted in every way, just as we are – yet he did not sin.'* (Hebrews 4:14) I will explain in great detail why these facts – that is, Jesus' dual natures and His sinless life – are so important in the next chapter when we look at His death, but I want to move on for now.

We have already read of Gabriel telling Mary that God would give Jesus *"the throne of David and He will reign over the house of Jacob forever, and of His kingdom there will be no end."* (Luke 1:32-33). So, let's explore further Jesus being the promised Messiah.

In those days, a decree went out from Caesar Augustus that all the world should be registered. This was the first registration when Quirinius was governor of Syria. And all went to be registered, each to his own town. (Luke 2:1-3)

On first reading, these sentences seem to be nothing more than trivial notes of history. However, the next verses show why they are significant.

And Joseph also went up from Galilee, from the town of Nazareth, to Judea, to the city of David, which is called Bethlehem, because he was of the house and lineage of David, to be registered with Mary, his betrothed, who was with child. (Luke 2:4-5)

I want to point out two things from these verses. First, notice that Joseph was from the Davidic line, the line from which the Messiah would come. Now, it is true that Joseph wasn't the biological father of Jesus. However, in the first-century Jewish culture, a person's lineage was determined by the father. Therefore, from a legal standpoint, Jesus was indeed a descendant of David, which qualified Him to be the Messiah. Secondly, notice the town in which Jesus was born, Bethlehem. Joseph and Mary were living close to a hundred miles to the north in the village of Nazareth, and, on the surface, it appears that it was only due to mundane political reasons that they would travel to the city of David. However, remember that in our previous chapter we read that the prophet Micah foretold that the Messiah would be born in Bethlehem (Micah 5:2). So, the decree from Caesar was clearly orchestrated by God. As Proverbs 21:1 states, *"The king's heart is a stream of water in the hand of the LORD; He turns it wherever He wills."* If God wanted Jesus to be born in Bethlehem, then He would have no problem making that happen.

After Jesus was born, an angel of the LORD appeared to some shepherds out in the fields and made this proclamation:

And the angel said to them, 'Fear not, for behold, I bring you good news of great joy that will be for all the people. For unto you is born this day in the city of David a Savior, who is Christ the Lord.' (Luke 2:10-11).

This angelic messenger of God made it unequivocally clear that Jesus was the promised Savior, the Messiah – or Christ in the Greek. Notice also that He would be for 'all the people.' This means that the good news of the Messiah's arrival wouldn't solely impact the Israelites. We'll touch on this important topic in more detail in just a moment.

After Jesus was born, his parents took Him to the temple in Jerusalem in order to fulfill a purification ritual found in the Mosaic Law. While there, they had an extraordinary encounter.

Now there was a man in Jerusalem, whose name was Simeon, and this man was righteous and devout, waiting for the consolation of Israel, and the Holy Spirit was upon him. And it had been revealed to him by the Holy Spirit that he would not see death before he had seen the Lord's Christ. And he came in the Spirit into the temple, and when the parents brought in the child Jesus, to do for him according to the custom of the Law, he took him up in his arms and praised God and said, 'Lord, now you are letting your servant depart in peace, according to your word; for my eyes have seen your salvation that you have prepared in the presence of all peoples, a light for revelation to the Gentiles, and for glory to your people Israel.' (Luke 2:25-32)

Just like the angel who had spoken to the shepherds, this second messenger from God was clearly claiming Jesus to be the Messiah. But also notice that the salvation that would come through Jesus would not just be for the Israelites. He would be *'a light for revelation to the Gentiles.'* The word 'Gentile' is how the Israelites referred to anyone who was not a Jew. So, this is actually an incredibly profound declaration. For millennia – ever since God had called Abraham out from Haran – the Israelites believed that they, and they alone, were God's chosen people. But here we read that Jesus would be a Savior for the entire world, which calls back to God's promise to Abraham in Genesis 12. *'I will bless those who bless you, and whoever curses you I will curse; and all the peoples on earth will be blessed through you.'* (Genesis 12:3) Jesus – the Messiah – would come from the line of Abraham, but He would not be the Savior for only Abraham's physical descendants. Once again, God was turning the expectations of the people upside down.

Simeon would continue speaking, saying to Mary, *'Behold, the child is appointed for the fall and rising of many in Israel, and for a sign that is opposed (and a sword will pierce through your own soul also), so that thoughts from many hearts may be revealed.'* (Luke 2:34-35)

Jesus was appointed by God the Father to bring about judgment – that is the 'fall' – of the prideful and rebellious, those who believe they have no need of God. But Jesus would also save – or cause the 'rising of' – all who humbly repent and receive Him as Lord and Savior. 'A sign that is opposed' was a foretelling of the intense opposition that Jesus would face, while the 'sword' to pierce Mary's soul most likely referred to the anguish that she would experience watching her son die on a Roman cross. And through it all, the thoughts of many hearts would be revealed. People then – just like today – would have to decide in their hearts if Jesus truly is the Messiah.

So far, we have seen three separate messengers from God – the angel, Gabriel; an unnamed angel who appeared to the shepherds; and Simeon – all proclaim Jesus as the Christ. But what did Jesus, Himself, claim?

The last section of Luke 2 contains a unique story in Jesus' life not told in the other three Gospels. When He was twelve years of age, He went to Jerusalem with His parents for the Passover Feast. However, His parents lost track of Him and began searching throughout the city. They eventually found Him in the temple, sitting amongst the teachers, both listening to them and answering their questions. When confronted by His mother, He answered, *'Why were you looking for me? Did you not know that I must be in my Father's house?'* (Luke 2:49) Some Bible scholars have translated Jesus' answer as, *'Did you not know that I must be about my Father's business?'* Regardless, though, of which translation is the most accurate, what can't be argued is that Jesus clearly viewed Himself as the Son of God. In fact, throughout all four Gospels, Jesus' claims about both His divinity and His role as the Messiah are unmistakable. He most commonly refers to Himself as the Son of Man, referencing Daniel's prophecy that we looked at in our previous chapter.

In my vision at night, I looked and there before me was one like a son of man, coming with the clouds of heaven. He approached the Ancient of Days and was led into his presence. He was given authority, glory and sovereign power; all nations and people of every language worshipped him. His dominion is an everlasting dominion that will not pass away, and his kingdom is one that will never be destroyed. (Daniel 7:13-14)

So, if Jesus was the promised Christ – the Anointed One of God, from the line of David, whose kingdom would be eternal – then He, like David, must have been a mighty warrior, right? As I've already mentioned, that's what the Israelites believed about the coming Messiah. But, no, Jesus' kingdom would not be military or political in nature at all. In fact, when Jesus stood before Pontius Pilate – the Roman governor over Judea – He told him, *'My kingdom is not of this world.'* (John 18:36) Christ's kingdom – at least for the time being – would be strictly a spiritual one.

I've claimed that God's plan of salvation can be seen through the ultimate and final establishing of His kingdom – defined as God's people, in God's place, under God's rule, enjoying God's blessing. So, how would Jesus go about establishing His spiritual kingdom? Well, firstly, it would not be confined to a limited, geographic location – neither within a certain area of land nor within a temple. Instead, it would reside in the hearts of His people. Wherever His people live in the world, there His kingdom will be. Secondly, as we have already seen, God's people in this new kingdom would not be limited to only Abraham's physical descendants. Jesus would be a Savior to the people of all the nations of the earth. Thirdly, God the Father would make a new covenant with His people. A covenant is simply an agreement between two parties in which they form a relationship that had not been present before. No longer would God's covenant be in any way tied to circumcision, the sacrificing of animals on an altar, or any of the other Old Testament laws. Rather, His new covenant would be tied to His Son, Jesus – specifically, His atoning, substitutionary death on the cross.

But Jesus wouldn't go directly to the cross. Instead, He would first have an earthly ministry in which He would teach the people about this new covenant. So, instead of wielding a literal sword to fight back His enemies, Jesus would use a spiritual sword. He would preach God's Word. This is how Mark describes the beginning of Jesus' ministry.

Now, after John was arrested, Jesus came into Galilee, proclaiming the Gospel of God and saying, 'The time is fulfilled. The kingdom of God is at hand. Repent and believe in the Gospel.' (Mark 1:15)

In this one verse, we can see the essence of Jesus' preaching. He was claiming that His arrival would begin to fulfill all of the Old Testament promises. Additionally, the reason that the kingdom of God was at hand was because He – the King – was now on the scene. And, finally, He gave a command: to repent and believe. To repent means to turn away from. To turn away from one's manner of thinking and living. But Biblical repentance is much more than that, for the truth is that millions of people 'repent' every January 1st when they make their New Year's resolutions. Biblical repentance, however, includes a turning towards, as well. But not turning towards a list of rules in order to find salvation. Rather, it involves a turning towards the saving work of Jesus. The second part of the command was to believe in the Gospel. But what Gospel? Well, the good news that Jesus is the promised Chosen One of God who would establish God's kingdom. His message was and still is quite simple. He was essentially saying, "I am the promised Messiah King who will save and lead God's people. Repent and believe the good news that I am who I say I am." That's it. Just repent and believe. Salvation can't get much easier than that. It's certainly easier than trying to obey the hundreds of commands found in the Mosaic Law.

While the primary focus of Jesus' ministry was preaching the Gospel, it wasn't the only aspect. Jesus also performed many amazing miracles – casting out demons, healing the sick and the lame, giving sight to the blind, calming the storms, and even raising the dead. As God, He possessed the power of God, and His miracles gave testimony to His divinity and to His claim that He was the Christ, God's Chosen One. As the apostle John writes, *'Jesus performed many other signs in the presence of his disciples, which are not recorded in this book. But these are written that you may believe that Jesus is the Messiah, the Son of God, and that by believing you may have life in his name.'* (John 20:30-31)

As you can imagine, someone with this type of power would draw a crowd, and Jesus certainly did. He traveled throughout the land, visiting towns and villages, preaching His Gospel, and wherever He went, crowds would gather. However, He also had an inner circle of followers – disciples – that He had called to Himself at the beginning of His ministry. They lived with Jesus for three years, learning from Him and seeing all of His miraculous signs. At one point, Jesus asked His disciples a very important question.

When Jesus came to the region of Caesarea Philippi, he asked his disciples, 'Who do the people say the Son of Man is?' They replied,

'Some say John the Baptist; others say Elijah; and still others, Jeremiah or one of the prophets.' 'But what about you?' he asked. 'Who do you say I am?' Simon Peter answered, 'You are the Messiah, the Son of the living God.' Jesus replied, 'Blessed are you, Simon son of Jonah, for this was not revealed to you by flesh and blood, but by my Father in heaven.' (Matthew 16:13-17)

    A lot of people were saying a lot of different things about Jesus. And it's no different today, is it? People make all kinds of claims about who He is. But Jesus wanted to know what His closest followers believed, and, before concluding this chapter, I would like to pose that same question. So far, we have read of many declarations regarding Jesus. Angels, prophets, the disciples of Jesus, and even Jesus Himself claimed that He is the Messiah, the Savior of the world. So, based on those claims, my question for you, dear reader, is, "Who do *you* say that Jesus is?" This is perhaps the most important question that you will ever answer, for it has eternal ramifications. I'll paraphrase C.S. Lewis' famous argument and state that saying that He was simply a good teacher is not a viable answer. According to Lewis, there are only three legitimate options from which you can choose. One, Jesus was a lunatic. A man out of His right mind who believed Himself to be God but wasn't. Two, He was liar. A man who knew that He wasn't God but falsely made that claim for evil purposes. Either way, though, lunatic or liar – Jesus can't simply be a 'good teacher' because good men don't tell lies and good teachers aren't insane. Or you can choose the third answer – believing that Jesus is who He says He is – the Son of God and the Christ who came to save the world. But choose wisely, for your decision will determine the eternal destination of your soul. Perhaps, the most famous verse in all of Scripture is John 3:16:

For God so loved the world that he gave his one and only Son, that whoever believes in him shall not perish but have eternal life.

    However, it's important to know that the verses that follow are just as significant:

For God did not send his Son into the world to condemn the world, but to save the world through him. Whoever believes in him is *not condemned, but <u>whoever does not believe stands condemned already because they have not believed in the name of God's one and only Son.</u>* (John 3:17-18)

    The apostle John is reiterating what the Scriptures make clear elsewhere – that we are sinners by nature and, therefore, our default status is condemnation. We are guilty of breaking God's holy commands and, because of that rebellion, we deserve to be separated from Him forever. But God the Father, out of love, sent His Son to save us from that condemnation, and in the next chapter, I will explain in detail how exactly Jesus would accomplish this saving work. For now, though, it's important to know that Jesus' gift of salvation doesn't come to us automatically. We must receive it. As Jesus commanded, we must repent and believe. We must repent of our sinful way of living and entrust our lives to Him in order to be saved. It is only through trusting in Jesus that we can be reconciled to God. If we do not receive Jesus as Lord and Savior, then the only other option is for us to remain in our condemned state. We will die in our sins, which will separate us from God for eternity. I may not personally know you, but I certainly don't want that for you. I pray that God will grant you the faith to believe.

Chapter 9: Jesus Dies (John 19)

We are now finally to what, I believe, is not only the pivotal moment in God's plan of salvation but also the pivotal moment in all of history – the death of Jesus. Before we examine why His death is so important, however, I would like to first look at the events that led up to it.

In the previous chapter, I mentioned that Jesus' earthly ministry consisted primarily of preaching the Gospel of God. He preached, among other things, that He was God's promised Messiah who would fulfill all of the Old Testament prophecies. If you're not familiar with the story, then it might be surprising to find out that almost all of the religious leaders of that time hated both Jesus and His message. These were prideful men who believed they were righteous due to both their ethnic heritage – that is, being a descendant of Abraham – and also to their adherence to the Mosaic Law. In fact, they loved their works-based self-righteousness so much that they added hundreds of their own oppressive rules to God's Law, perverting His commands and statutes into something that they were never meant to be. But these religious leaders had no actual love of God in their hearts, which as you may recall was God's primary command.

'You shall love the LORD your God with all your heart and with all your soul and with all your might.' (Deuteronomy 6:5)

The religious leaders' animus towards Jesus was exacerbated by the fact that He constantly rebuked them, calling them snakes, white-washed tombs, and even sons of the devil. Jesus didn't pull His punches, did He? So, they hated Him because He called out their hypocrisy, their greed, and their misuse of God's Word. They hated Him because, in their eyes, He dismissed the Law. They hated Him because He taught with authority and, therefore, drew crowds that they could not. And they hated Him because He claimed to be divine, putting Himself on equal footing to both God and to the commands found in Scripture. They considered His claim to be blasphemy, which in that culture carried the penalty of death. And, due to their hatred, they called for Pontius Pilate – the Roman governor of Judea – to kill Him. But Pilate was initially hesitant to do so.

Once more Pilate came out and said to the Jews gathered there, 'Look, I am bringing him [Jesus] out to you to let you know that I find no basis for a charge against him.' (John 19:4)

Pilate had spoken to Jesus but had not found Him guilty of any crime, but the Jewish leaders didn't care.

As soon as the chief priests and their officials saw him, they shouted, 'Crucify! Crucify!' But Pilate answered, 'You take him and crucify him. As for me, I find no basis for the charge against him.' The Jewish leaders insisted, 'We have a law, and according to that law he must die, because he claimed to be the Son of God.' (John 19:6-7)

Crucifixion was one of the Romans' favorite forms of punishment, and it was incredibly painful. It is, in fact, where we get our word 'excruciating.' And that's what these Jewish leaders demanded be done to Jesus. The next verses state that Pilate tried to set Jesus free, but the Jewish leaders would not hear of it. Eventually, Pilate gave in.

Finally, Pilate handed him over to them to be crucified. (John 19:16)

So, Jesus – having already been severely flogged – was taken outside of the city of Jerusalem and was crucified. Peter, in Acts 2:3, states that Jesus was actually nailed to the cross. I can't imagine the pain. Large, metal spikes pierced His hands and feet, driving through muscle and bones and ligaments, pinning His battered and bruised body to those wooden beams. And He would hang there until He finally died.

When he had received the drink, Jesus said, 'It is finished.' With that, he bowed his head and gave up his spirit. (John 19:30)

Afterwards, one of the Roman soldiers verified that Jesus had actually died.

Now, it was the day of Preparation, and the next day was to be a special Sabbath. Because the Jewish leaders did not want the bodies left on the crosses during the Sabbath, they asked Pilate to have the legs broken and the bodies taken down. The soldiers, therefore, came and broke the legs of the first man who had been crucified with Jesus and then those of the other. But when they came to Jesus and found that he was already dead, they did not break his legs. Instead, one of the soldiers pierced Jesus' side with a spear, bringing a sudden flow of blood and water. (John 19:31-34)

Not only did Jesus die, but His blood was shed, as well. The chapter ends with Jesus' corpse being buried in a nearby tomb.

So, all of that explains why Jesus died – at least, it does so from an earthly perspective. But what exactly did His death have to do with God's plan of salvation? To understand that, I need to remind you of a few principles and prophecies that we've already examined throughout this study.

Back in chapter five, I introduced what I believe is one of the most important principles found in the Bible: God's plan of salvation would involve substitution. I then went on to explain that the Old Testament sacrificial system could never fully satisfy God's just demand that sin be punished because bulls and goats, even ones without blemish, simply don't have the same inherent value as humans since we, and we alone, were originally made in the image of God. Therefore, unless we wanted to continue sacrificing animals until the end of time, we needed a better substitute. A substitute that – at a minimum – possessed the same value as humanity, but also one who was sinless. Because the death of an ordinary man – born with a sinful human nature, inherited from Adam – could only ever pay off his own life-debt to the holy Judge of the universe. His death would never be sufficient enough to pay the penalty of his sins and those of anyone else. But where in the world could one possibly find a sinless man? It was, clearly, an impossible scenario.

Well, God loves making the impossible happen, and this is where the dual natures of Jesus – Him being both fully God and fully man – come into play. God's plan of salvation involved God Himself paying the penalty of our sins. He would be our substitute and pay our life-debt. For only God is sinless. Only God is holy and pure and perfect. But there was one problem, though – the consequence of sin is death, and God cannot die. He is eternal. So, what would He do? His solution was to take on a form that could die. So, God – specifically, the Son of God – voluntarily humbled Himself by stepping down from His eternal throne in Heaven and taking on human flesh. Jesus was both fully God and fully human, both sinless and also capable of dying.

I honestly cannot get my mind wrapped around what He did for us – what it must have been like for the glorious God of the universe to become human. My analogy obviously falls way short, but it would have to be similar to a young, beautiful, rich, powerful, famous world leader willingly taking on the form of a dung-beetle. That sacrifice alone is amazing enough. What's even more amazing, though, is that, after taking on that lowly form, He would then be willing to die in our place. But, as we have read, He did that very thing. Jesus, who had already humbled Himself by simply putting on our flesh, would humble Himself further by letting His creation – proud, sinful, rebellious men – kill Him in one of the most painful ways imaginable. He is the suffering servant about whom Isaiah prophesied.

'He was despised and rejected by men, a man of sorrows and acquainted with grief; and as one from whom men hide their faces, he was despised and we esteemed him not. Surely, he has born our griefs and carried our sorrows; yet we esteemed him stricken, smitten by God, and afflicted. But he was pierced for our transgressions; he was crushed for our iniquities; upon him was the chastisement that brought us peace, and with his wounds we are healed. All we like sheep have gone astray; we have turned – every one – to his own way; and the LORD laid on him the iniquity of us all.' (Isaiah 53:3-6)

It was on a Roman cross that the sinless Jesus died. To most people watching, He died due to blasphemy. But, in reality, He willingly died in order to fulfill His Father's plan of salvation. That is why, on the cross, as He died, He proclaimed, *'It is finished.'* (John 19:30) He died as humanity's substitute – taking on our sins and the accompanying guilt and then paying the penalty of those sins so that we would not have to. The Old Testament sacrifices of bulls and goats could only temporarily deal with our guilt. Therefore, they had to be repeated over and over. But they were simply a foreshadowing, pointing forward to the perfect sacrifice that was to come. Jesus' sacrifice was one time for all time. As the Son of God, His life possessed infinite value, worth more than the lives of every human being combined. Therefore, His death was sufficient enough to cover the life-debt owed by all of humanity – past, present, and future. Now, that does not mean that every person actually has been saved from the penalty of their sins, because not all have faith. Not all believe. And, as Jesus commanded, we must repent and believe. If we do not – by faith – receive His gift of salvation, then we will have no other option but to pay off our life-debt ourselves. I have made my decision. Which option will you choose?

In chapter five, I asked how it was possible for God to be both just and merciful at the same time since those two qualities are completely opposed to one another. Well, the cross of Christ answers that question. At the cross, Jesus took on our sins, and then God the Father displayed His holy, righteous justice to the world by pouring out His just wrath on those sins. That explains why Jesus, on the cross, would cry out, *"My God, my God, why have you forsaken me?"* (Matthew 27:46). Because, remember, sin separates us from God. So, in that moment, in a way that I can't truly explain, the triune God was separated from Himself. The Son was alienated from His Father. And I believe it was that part of His sacrifice – His separation from His Father – more than the physical pain that He would endure, which had caused Jesus to be so full of anguish the night before in the Garden of Gethsemane. He had told His disciples, *'My soul is overwhelmed with sorrow to the point of death. Stay here and keep watch with me.'* (Matthew 26:38) Jesus' gift of salvation may be free to you and me, but it wasn't free for Him. It cost Him dearly.

But what would compel God – the Father and the Son – to go through with such a costly and painful sacrifice? They certainly didn't have to. No one was forcing them. The answer – it was His unfathomable love.

But God demonstrates his own love for us in this: While we were still sinners, Christ died for us. (Romans 5:8)

Therefore, the cross wasn't simply where God displayed His justice to the world. It was also where He displayed His amazing, merciful love by being our substitute, by taking our sin and the penalty that comes with it upon Himself. The cross is where God's justice and mercy met. How amazing is our God.

With all of that being said, in spite of how significant Jesus' sacrificial, atoning, substitutionary death was, it is, in fact, not the end of the story. Believe it or not, God's plan of salvation gets even better, but I will save that for the next chapter.

Chapter 10: Jesus Lives & the Holy Spirit Indwells (Luke 24)

In full disclosure, I will not be focusing solely on one passage of Scripture in this chapter. I am going to 'cheat' a bit, and the reason is because I have a tremendous amount of material to cover. Therefore, while I am going to start off by primarily focusing on the verses in Luke 24, I will end up traveling all over the Bible in order to adequately explain this penultimate portion of God's plan of salvation. Anyway, with that confession out of the way, let's begin.

In the previous chapter, we examined God's immeasurable mercy as seen in Jesus' atoning, substitutionary sacrifice on the cross. By His death and the shedding of His blood, we can receive salvation – the forgiveness of sins and reconciliation with our Creator. It is an amazing story of God's love for the world. If you are not familiar with the story, then you might think that it ends here, for Jesus, the promised Messiah, has died. And death typically marks the end to a person's story. Jesus' closest followers certainly thought it was the end. After His crucifixion, they in fact went into hiding, believing that the religious leaders would call for their deaths next.

On the evening of that first day of the week, when the disciples were together, with the doors locked for fear of the Jewish leaders... (John 20:19a)

I can only imagine what they must have been feeling. For three years, they had lived with Jesus, watching Him perform amazing miracles. They saw with their own eyes the power of God on display in this incredible man, which gave testimony to His divinity and to His claim that He was the Christ, God's Chosen One. As such, His followers believed that He would soon push the Romans out of their Promised Land and restore the kingdom of Israel to its former glory. And then, suddenly, it's all over. Jesus is dead and buried in a tomb. The text states that they were fearful, but they had to have been filled with disappointment, confusion, and despair as well. For all of their hopes had died with Christ, and there are very few things in this world that are worse than feeling hopeless. But the truth is that they shouldn't have been. For Jesus didn't simply perform miracles during His earthly ministry. As we saw in chapter eight, He also preached. And part of that preaching was explicitly telling His disciples what would happen to Him.

Jesus took the Twelve aside and told them, 'We are going up to Jerusalem, and everything that is written by the prophets about the Son of Man will be fulfilled. He will be delivered over to the Gentiles. They will mock him, insult him and spit on him; they will flog him and kill him. On the third day, he will rise again.' (Luke 18:31-33)

His words seem incredibly straight-forward and clear. So, how could the disciples not understand? To make matters worse, this is actually the third time that it is recorded in the Gospel according to Luke that Jesus had predicted His death and resurrection to His followers. So, how could they forget such an important promise from Him? Before we judge them too harshly, let's read the next verse.

The disciples did not understand any of this. Its meaning was hidden from them, and they did not know what he was talking about. (Luke 18:34)

The text doesn't say who hid the meaning of Jesus' message or why it was hidden. I assume that it was God, Himself, who did it, but that is pure speculation on my part. Ultimately, it doesn't matter. It's not a plain thing or a main thing. What is most important is that Jesus predicted that He would rise from the dead, and in the following verses, we will see that He spoke the truth. For He is God, which means that He can only speak truth.

On the first day of the week, very early in the morning, the women took the spices they had prepared and went to the tomb. They found the stone rolled away from the tomb, but when they entered, they did not find the body of the Lord Jesus. While they were wondering about this, suddenly two men in clothes that gleamed like lightning stood beside them. In their fright, the women bowed down with their faces to the ground, but the men said to them, <u>'Why do you look for the living among the dead? He is not here. He has risen! Remember</u>

how he told you, while he was still with you in Galilee: 'The Son of Man must be delivered over to the hand of sinners, be crucified and on the third day be raised again.'' Then they remembered his words. (Luke 24:1-8)

Can you imagine the excitement that these women must have felt? Wellsprings of hope must have burst forth from their souls. They returned to the disciples who were still in hiding – I'm betting they ran the entire way back – and told them of what they had seen and heard at the tomb.

But they did not believe the women, because their words seemed to them like nonsense. (Luke 24:11)

One of the things that I love about the Bible is its honesty. It possesses an incredible authenticity, with Jesus' followers shown warts and all. We read of them routinely being fearful, lacking faith, not understanding Jesus' teachings, and even denying that they know Him. In the Gospels, they do not come off looking good at all, which is great. It means that I can relate to them. And, here, we read of them not believing the testimony of the women.

So, Jesus, because He is merciful and kind, to deal with the disciples' doubts and confusion, appeared to them Himself. He first met and spoke with two of His followers on the road to Emmaus (Luke 24:13-35), and then He appeared to His inner group in Jerusalem.

While they [the disciples] *were still talking about this, Jesus himself stood among them and said to them, 'Peace be with you.'* (Luke 24:36)

Jesus' words were more than just a greeting. They were a declaration of who He is and what He had achieved. Due to His atoning sacrifice, God's wrath towards sin had been satisfied, thereby ending the alienation between humanity and God. Therefore, these men now had peace with God through Christ. Jesus was their peace, and He was with them.

After easing their fears that they were seeing a ghost, Jesus then proceeded to do what He does better than anyone else – preach God's Word.

He said to them, 'This is what I told you while I was still with you: Everything must be fulfilled that is written about me in the Law of Moses, the Prophets, and the Psalms.' <u>Then, he opened their minds so they could understand the Scriptures.</u> He told them: 'This is what is written: The Messiah will suffer and rise from the dead on the third day, and repentance for the forgiveness of sins will be preached in his name to all the nations, beginning at Jerusalem. You are witnesses of these things.' (Luke 24:44-48)

Jesus didn't simply pop back up and say, "Surprise, I'm here!" No, like the wonderful teacher that He is, He took His disciples back to the Holy Scriptures in order to explain to them exactly how and why everything had transpired. And we can see why He did that. He was about to commission them to go out to all the nations and preach repentance for the forgiveness of sins that can only be found through Him. While these disciples were eyewitnesses to Jesus' resurrection, the people who would hear this good news – including those of us today – would not be. Meaning that our faith in Jesus as the Christ would not be based upon what we can see with our eyes. It would be based upon the truths found in Scripture. Therefore, it was imperative that these disciples actually understood the Bible so that they could, then, preach it to the lost, broken, and unsaved people of the world.

Before continuing, I'd like to pause here for a moment to comment on the importance of the resurrection. As amazing as Jesus' sacrificial death is, it is actually His resurrection that gives Christianity validity as a belief system, and here is why. As we have seen, the Old Testament prophecies stated that the Messiah's kingdom would be eternal. Additionally, Jesus, Himself, promised His followers that He would rise on the third day. Had God the Father not resurrected His Son, then that would have proven both Jesus and all of the Old Testament prophets to be liars and, therefore, would have invalidated all of the Messianic prophecies and everything that Jesus had said and done. If Jesus was still in the grave, then He would be no different than every other religious leader throughout human history. It is only because He is alive – and because we have the written accounts of men who saw Him resurrected – that we can truly have faith in Him as the Christ.

And, while we're on the topic of faith in the resurrection, I know that I said back in chapter two that I would not dive into the realm of apologetics, but please indulge me briefly while I state that it is the disciples' behavior as recorded in the Scriptures that, in my mind, proves the resurrection occurred. As we have seen, after Jesus' arrest and crucifixion, these men were terrified and went into hiding, for they believed that the religious leaders would come after them next. But, if you read the book of Acts, you will discover a miraculous turn-around. These men, who had been terrified, were suddenly preaching the name of Jesus boldly – without fear of death – in public at the temple. In fact, they even preached Jesus as the Christ to the very same religious leaders who had conspired to have Jesus killed. What in the world could legitimately and logically explain this incredible display of bravery other than the fact that these men had seen the resurrected Christ and realized that this world and this life are not all that there is? Now, had it only been one disciple who was recklessly preaching the name of Jesus, then you might could convince me that he was simply insane and was willing to risk his life due to his delusions. But it wasn't just one of the disciples. It was all of them. And no one will ever convince me that they all suffered from the exact same psychosis. Nor will anyone ever convince me that these men simply lied about the resurrection. For I don't know of anyone who is willing to die – which most of these men did – for something that they know is a lie. For me to actually believe that, I would have to completely turn off the logical, reasoning part of my brain, which, ironically, is the exact thing of which we Christians are routinely accused. Anyway, that's my short apologia. Let's now get back to God's plan of salvation.

After appearing to the disciples, Jesus shared with them some important information:

'I am going to send you what my Father has promised; but stay in the city until you have been clothed with power from on high.' (Luke 24:25)

To understand what promise Jesus is referencing, we will be looking at the Gospel according to John, where Jesus makes multiple promises to His disciples. But before we get there, let's go ahead and finish reading the final verses of Luke 24.

When he had led them out to the vicinity of Bethany, he lifted up his hands and blessed them. While he was blessing them, he left them and was taken up to heaven. Then, they worshipped him and returned to Jerusalem with great joy. And they stayed continually at the temple, praising God. (Luke 24:50-53)

After Jesus was resurrected, He spent about forty days with His disciples, encouraging them and continuing to teach them. And, then, He returned to Heaven, to His rightful place at the right hand of His Father. However, before He left, He made some promises that we will look at now.

'If you love me, keep my commands. And I will ask the Father, and he will give you another advocate to help you and be with you forever – the Spirit of truth. The world cannot accept him because it neither sees him nor knows him. But you know him, for he lives with you and will be in you. I will not leave you as orphans; I will come to you.' (John 14:15-18)

Prior to these verses, Jesus had explained to His disciples that He was going to leave them, referencing His ascension back into Heaven. But He promised them that, even though He was leaving, they would not be left alone – that is, left as orphans. He would send the third member of the Trinity – the Holy Spirit – to be with them and to live inside of them forever. The implication of this event is so staggering that I must take a bit of time to explain its importance.

At the conclusion of the previous chapter, I stated that Jesus' death wasn't the end to God's plan of salvation and that the story would actually get better. But Jesus' resurrection is not the only way the story improves. As we read in the verses above, Jesus promised that the Father would send us an Advocate to live within us. Meaning that Jesus didn't come to earth and die on our behalf simply to save us *from* punishment – that is, God's wrath and Hell. He also came to save us *into* a blessing – specifically, into a relationship with Himself. However, with Jesus being in Heaven, it would be rather difficult to have a great relationship with Him, right? Well, this is where the Holy Spirit comes into play. I mentioned previously that Jesus' kingdom would be a spiritual kingdom – at least for the time being. His kingdom would reside in the hearts of His people. Therefore, from that point on, God Himself, the Holy Spirit, would come to live inside of all of His people. That is absolutely mind blowing. That the holy, pure, perfect Creator God of the universe is willing to come dwell inside of a wretch like me. I truly can't get my mind wrapped around that. But, wait, it gets even better. The relationship between God and His people isn't cold and distant. It's not the relationship of a stern monarch sitting high above his lowly slaves. It's the relationship between a Father and His children. The apostle Paul explains:

For those who are led by the Spirit of God are the children of God. The Spirit you received does not make you slaves, so that you live in fear again; rather the Spirit you received brought about your adoption to sonship. And by him we cry, 'Abba, Father.' The Spirit Himself testifies with our spirit that we are God's children. (Romans 8:14-16)

How absolutely wonderful. Through faith in Christ, I am an adopted and loved child of God. That is my ultimate identity. No matter what may happen in my life, no matter how my earthly circumstances may change, my identity as God's child will always remain. Whether I'm married or divorced, young or old, rich or poor, healthy or sick, my identity as His child will never change.

But God's blessings get even better. Not only do we get a relationship with God the moment we receive Jesus as Lord and Savior, but that relationship will actually last for eternity. The promise of eternal life can be seen throughout the Scriptures, but I'll take you to just one example. At one point in His ministry, Jesus was teaching His followers that He is the 'Good Shepherd,' clearly referencing the prophecies found in both Isaiah 40 and Ezekiel 34. He then makes this promise:

'My sheep listen to my voice; I know them, and they follow me. <u>I give them eternal life, and they shall never perish; no one will snatch them out of my hand. My Father, who has given them to me, is greater than all; no one can snatch them out of my Father's hand.</u> I and the Father are one.' (John 10:27-30)

I stated above that I am a loved and adopted child of God through faith in Christ. That is my ultimate identity. Nothing will ever change that. And, here, we see that even my physical death won't change the fact that I am His son. God will be my Father for eternity. What an amazing promise that gives me incredible comfort and peace. I have peace knowing that the death of my physical body is not the end. It is only a portal into a better existence. As Alistair Begg once said, "Once we've settled this issue of death as Christians, what else is there really to worry about?" That is so true.

But what role does the Holy Spirit play in this promise of eternal life? Well, not only does He testify with our spirit that we are God's children, but, as the apostle Paul explains, the Spirit's presence within the believer is a guarantee that we will inherit God's eternal kingdom.

When you believed, you were marked in him [Jesus] *with a seal, the promised Holy Spirit, who is a deposit guaranteeing our inheritance until the redemption of those who are God's possession – to the praise of his glory.* (Ephesians 1:13-14)

So, the Holy Spirit both testifies to our sonship and also acts as a guarantee to our eternal inheritance. But that is not all that He does. He fulfills many other tasks, such as convicting us of our sin, leading us into truth, blessing us with a variety of spiritual gifts, and interceding on our behalf when we don't even know what we should pray. However, there is one other specific role that He fulfills that I want to focus on now. Remember what Jesus said to His disciples after first appearing to them after His resurrection:

'I am going to send you what my Father has promised; but stay in the city until <u>you have been clothed with power from on high.</u>' (Luke 24:25)

The Holy Spirit would infuse or 'clothe' Jesus' followers with power, which calls us back to that mysterious promise that we looked at in chapter five of this study, the mysterious promise spoken by Moses in Deuteronomy.

Before we read that promise again, though, let me remind you of the framework that we have been using throughout this study as we have explored God's plan of salvation – the kingdom of God. We defined it as God's people, in God's place, under God's rule, enjoying God's blessing. God's new kingdom revolves around Jesus and is, currently, spiritual in nature. God's people are those who have entrusted their lives to Jesus as the Christ, the Savior who takes away the sins of the world. God's place is in the hearts of His people, by the indwelling of the Holy Spirit. And God's blessing can be seen in a variety of ways but, primarily, through the loving, eternal relationship that we have with Him as our Heavenly Father. But what about 'under God's rule?' This is the one area that has tripped up God's people over and over throughout history. Adam and Eve rebelled against God's rule in the Garden of Eden, and the Israelites repeatedly forsook God and broke His covenant in the Promised Land. Due to our sinful natures, we keep spoiling God's kingdom. So, what did God promise that He would do?

'And the LORD your God will circumcise your heart and the heart of your offspring, so that you will love the LORD your God with all your heart and with all your soul, that you may live.' (Deuteronomy 30:6)

Our hearts are naturally sinful. Therefore, God promised that He would deal with our heart issue by spiritually circumcising it. And, as we shall see, He didn't just make this promise to Moses but to other Old Testament prophets, as well.

'<u>I will give them an undivided heart and put a new spirit in them;</u> <u>I will remove from them their heart of stone and give them a heart of</u>

flesh. Then, they will follow my decrees and be careful to keep my laws. They will be my people and I will be their God.' (Ezekiel 11:19)

'This is the covenant I will make with the people of Israel after that time,' declares the LORD. 'I will put my law in their minds and write it on their hearts. I will be their God, and they will be my people. No longer will they teach their neighbor, or say to one another, "Know the LORD," because they will all know me, from the least of them to the greatest,' declares the LORD. 'For I will forgive their wickedness and will remember their sins no more.' (Jeremiah 31:33-34)

'I will give them a heart to know me, that I am the LORD. They will be my people, and I will be their God, for they will return to me with all their heart.' (Jeremiah 24:7)

God promised to circumcise our hearts; to give us an undivided heart; to remove our hearts of stone; to write His law on our hearts; and to give us a new heart capable of knowing Him. And how would He go about accomplishing this? By giving us *His* heart, the Holy Spirit. Just as God redeemed the Israelites out of literal slavery in Egypt, He now, by the Holy Spirit, saves His people from spiritual slavery by breaking the chains that bind us to our sinful natures. As the apostle Paul states in his letter to the Christians in Rome, while sin may still remain within us, the presence and power of the Holy Spirit has set us free from its tyrannical reign in our lives.

We were therefore buried with him [Jesus] through baptism into death in order that, just as Christ was raised from the dead through the glory of the Father, we too may live a new life. For if we have been united with him in a death like his, we will certainly also be united with him in a resurrection like his. For we know that our old self was crucified with him so that the body ruled by sin might be done away with, that we should no longer be slaves to sin – because anyone who has died has been set free from sin....Therefore, do not let sin reign in your mortal body so that you obey its evil desires. (Romans 6:4-7, 12)

Jesus' promise of eternal life doesn't solely consist of a future dimension. This new life – free from the tyranny of sin – begins the moment we believe, empowered by the Holy Spirit. Now, this does not mean that those of us in Christ no longer struggle with sin, for our sinful nature is still present, and it still demands its own way. Therefore, there is now an ongoing and irreconcilable war taking place inside the followers of Jesus. Any Christian who is being honest will admit to this fact. But what the indwelling of the Sprit does mean for us is that we are no longer spiritually dead, existing in a dominion of darkness with sin as our master. We now have a new Master and the freedom to choose the better way – God's way – and to walk in the newness of life. The indwelling Holy Spirit progressively saves us from the power of sin, which allows us to willingly and lovingly submit to God's rule. We don't do it perfectly – at least for the time being. But, with the presence of the Spirit, we at least now have the desire to do so.

So, as we can see, God's plan of salvation never truly involved restoring the Israelite kingdom in the Promised Land. That kingdom was only a model of what was to come, a foreshadowing of God's spiritual kingdom that now encompasses the four corners of the earth. And, if you read Ephesians 1 – which I will let you do on your own – then you can see the Trinity at work in establishing this spiritual kingdom. God the Father planned our salvation from eternity past, before He had even created the world; God the Son procured this salvation for us through His substitutionary, atoning death on the cross; and the Holy Spirit, through His indwelling, both applies and empowers this salvation in the hearts of His people. Those of us in Christ are God's people, in God's place, under God's rule, enjoying God's blessing.

However, the story of the Bible – the story of God's plan of salvation – is not quite yet finished. For, as wonderful as His current spiritual kingdom is, there are still some problems with it. Problems that God will decisively and ultimately deal with once and for all. We will explore these imperfections and how He is going to eradicate them in our final chapter.

Chapter 11: God's Perfect Kingdom (Revelation 20-22)

In our previous chapter, I explained how God has established His spiritual kingdom. A kingdom that He is still expanding even today with every new, lost soul that He saves – by His grace, through faith in His Son, empowered by the indwelling of His Spirit. The story of the Bible is not complete, however, because, despite how wonderful God's current kingdom is, it is still not perfect. As the Scriptures reveal, God is pure and holy, meaning that His final kingdom must be pure and holy, as well. He will not tolerate any imperfections. In this last chapter of our study, we will discover how He is going to eradicate these imperfections by looking at Revelation, the last book of the Bible.

If this news causes some of you to grimace, I completely understand, for Revelation can be difficult to understand. I would argue that the Bible is the most misunderstood, misused, and misrepresented book in all of the world, and, of its sixty-six books, Revelation is probably the letter that causes the most confusion. However, I believe that where most people go wrong is by not taking a 'big picture' approach. The book is full of mysterious, veiled prophetic visions and, therefore, if we get bogged down in the weeds, trying to understand the meaning of every detail of every vision, I believe that we will quickly lose our way. I think a much better approach is simply to focus on the main principles found within the book. And, in my opinion, the main principle of Revelation is that, in the end, God wins. He is all-powerful, sovereign, and in control. Nothing and no one can prevail against His plans. If we hold onto that primary truth, then all of the mysterious details that surround it, ultimately, fade into the background and, therefore, no longer cause confusion. So, with that in mind, let's begin.

In the Garden of Eden, we saw God bring forth His creation. And while the Scriptures state that His creation was 'very good,' in truth it was perfect. Adam and Eve shared perfect intimacy with each other, with nature around them and, most importantly, with their Creator. However, God's creation didn't stay perfect. Evil – in the form of the devil, the serpent – entered the scene. Soon after, God's people sinned, which was quickly followed by the devastating consequences of that sin, with the worst curse being death. Well, those three imperfections – evil, sin, and death – are still present today in God's spiritual kingdom. And if you're thinking, "Really, you actually believe that Evil – with a capital E – exists? Sin and death – okay, I'll admit to those. But you truly think that the devil exists in our world?" My answer is, "Yes. I believe it because the Scriptures claim it." The Bible is clear that Satan and his demons are real.

The apostle Paul wrote the following to the Christians in Ephesus:

Finally, be strong in the Lord and in his mighty power. Put on the full armor of God, so that you can take your stand against the devil's schemes. For our struggle is not against flesh and blood, but against the rulers, against the authorities, against the powers of this dark world, and against the spiritual forces of evil in the heavenly realms. (Ephesians 6:10-13)

But Paul is not the only apostle to preach this truth. Peter, too, makes the same claim.

Be alert and of sober mind. Your enemy the devil prowls around like a roaring lion looking for someone to devour. Resist him, standing firm in the faith, because you know that the family of believers throughout the world is undergoing the same kind of sufferings. (1 Peter 5:8-9)

And, finally, we can read of Jesus' brother, James, affirm the existence of the evil one.

Submit yourselves, then, to God. Resist the devil, and he will flee from you. (James 4:7)

So, the Bible is clear – the devil exists. And with that out of the way, let's now examine how God is going to consummate His perfect kingdom by eradicating the three remaining imperfections, starting with sin. In Revelation, God gives the apostle John a vision of the end-times, and this is what he writes:

After this, I looked, and there before me was a great multitude that no one could count, from every nation, tribe, people and language, standing before the throne and before the Lamb. They were wearing white robes and were holding palm branches in their hands. And they cried out in a loud voice, 'Salvation belongs to our God, who sits on the throne, and to the Lamb.' (Revelation 7:9-10)

Here, John is reiterating what we have already learned in this study – that God's kingdom is not simply for Abraham's physical descendants. His people will come from all the nations. In this vision, the apostle sees God's people worshiping both God the Father and His Son – the perfect sacrificial Lamb, who died on the cross to take away the sins of the world. Additionally, God's people will be wearing white robes. But what do these robes signify exactly? A few verses later, an elder explains their meaning to John.

And he said, 'These are they who have come out of the great tribulation; they have washed their robes and made them white in the blood of the Lamb.' (Revelation 7:14)

The whiteness of the robes – washed clean through the sacrifice of Christ – signifies purity and righteousness. Meaning that, in Heaven, we will finally be without sin. The irreconcilable war taking place inside of Christ's believers will finally end because our sinful natures will be dealt with once and for all. The apostle Paul explained how this can be to the Christians in Corinth when discussing the resurrection of our new bodies on the day that Jesus finally returns from Heaven.

But someone will ask, 'How are the dead raised? With what kind of body do they come?' You foolish person! What you sow does not come to life unless it dies.... So it is with the resurrection of the dead. What is sown [our body in the likeness of sinful Adam] *is perishable; what is raised is imperishable. It is sown in dishonor; it is raised in glory; It is sown in weakness; it is raised in power. It is sown a natural body; it is raised a spiritual body. Thus, it is written, 'The first man Adam became a living being;' the last Adam* [Jesus] *became a life-giving spirit.... As was the first man* [Adam] *of dust, so also are those who are of the dust, and <u>as is the man of heaven</u>* [Jesus]<u>, *so also are those who are of heaven*</u>. *Just as we have born the image of the man of dust, <u>we shall also bear the image of the man of heaven</u>.* (1 Corinthians 15:35-36, 42-45, 48-49)

Paul states that our glorified, imperishable, resurrected bodies will bear the image of Jesus, the man of Heaven. Just as Adam was made in the image of God and, therefore, was originally pure and without sin, so then we too – when we are resurrected in the image of the sinless Jesus – will be pure and without sin, as well, and praise God for that.

Therefore, in the Bible we can see a past, present, and future aspect to salvation; or three different 'types' of salvation, if you will. At the cross, Jesus saved us from the *penalty* of sin – past tense. During our lives, the Holy Spirit sanctifies us day by day – progressively saving us from the *power* of sin – present tense. And, lastly, when we are finally face-to-face with our Lord, He will save us from the *presence* of sin – future tense. And how amazing that will be. To finally be in His presence without my sinful nature interfering with my intimacy with Him. That truly will be Heaven.

So, from the Scriptures, we have read of how God will eradicate sin from His resurrected people. Let's continue in order to see how He will deal with the other two imperfections – evil and death. The later chapters of Revelation state that there will be a final battle between good and evil – between God and Satan, between God and all of those who oppose Him.

When the thousand years are over, Satan will be released from his prison and will go out to deceive the nations in the four corners of the earth – Gog and Magog – and to gather them for battle. In number they are like the sand on the seashore. They marched across the breadth of the earth and surrounded the camps of God's people, the city he loves. But fire came down from heaven and devoured them. And the devil, who deceived them, was thrown into the lake of burning sulfur, where the beast and the false prophets had been thrown. They will be tormented day and night forever and ever. (Revelation 20:7-10)

If we don't allow ourselves to get sidetracked by all of the details found in these verses and simply focus on the main idea, then we can see that God will defeat Satan and all of his followers. And, most importantly, it will be a complete and final victory. One that will last forever and ever. That is the second imperfection eradicated, and praise God for that, as well.

But the prophetic message doesn't end there. The next verses tell of a final day of judgment. It is a chilling promise where all the souls of everyone who has ever lived will stand before the holy, righteous Judge of the universe. Those who have not received eternal life through faith in Christ will be cast into a mysterious lake of fire. I don't know exactly what this lake of fire is. I don't know if the writer is being literal or is simply using poetic imagery. However, I believe that the main principle to grasp is that these non-believers will be cast out of God's presence for eternity. Based on the totality of the Scriptures, there is no doubt in my mind about that. However, God is not finished.

Then, death and Hades were thrown into the lake of fire. The lake of fire is the second death. (Revelation 20:14)

Here, we can see God eradicating death itself from His final kingdom.

As the apostle Paul wrote, *'For as in Adam all die, so also in Christ shall all be made alive. But each in his own order: Christ, the firstfruits; then at his coming, those who belong to Christ. Then comes the end, when he delivers the kingdom to God the Father after destroying every ruler and every authority and power. For he must reign until he has put all his enemies under his feet. <u>The last enemy to be destroyed is death.</u>'* (1 Corinthians 15:22-26)

Therefore, in the end, God's people will live with Him for eternity and will finally be free from the presence of both sin and evil. God truly is worthy of praise.

The last two chapters of Revelation tell us of how God, with the destruction of His last three enemies – evil, sin, and death – will finally bring forth His perfect kingdom. Unlike the silly tales you may have seen in Hollywood movies or Saturday morning cartoons, God's final kingdom in not going to be ethereal, with us floating up in the clouds, playing a harp. He is, in fact, going to create a new physical kingdom on a new and redeemed earth.

Then I saw 'a new heaven and a new earth,' for the first heaven and the first earth had passed away, and there was no longer any sea. I saw the Holy City, the new Jerusalem, coming down out of heaven from God, prepared as a bride beautifully dressed for her husband. (Revelation 21:1-2)

Our current universe, under God's curse due to the original sin of Adam and Eve, will be redeemed. A new heaven and earth – free of sin, decay, and death – will come in its place, and this new city – the bride – signifies all of God's redeemed people prepared for our Savior, Jesus. God will bring final and complete redemption – salvation – to both His people and to all of nature, which brings us to the end of the story of the Bible.

I would like to conclude this study by simply sharing a few final passages from Revelation. I am going to refrain from adding any more of my own commentary because I believe that the verses need no explanation. But I want to end with them because they contain amazing promises of God's perfect kingdom. Promises that fill me with hope and peace and joy. I pray that you will find them as equally comforting.

And I heard a loud voice from the throne saying, 'Look! God's dwelling place is now among the people, and he will dwell with them. They will be his people, and God himself with be with them and be their God. He will wipe every tear from their eyes. There will be no more death or mourning or crying or pain, for the old order of things has passed away.' (Revelation 21:3-4)

I did not see a temple in the city, because the Lord God Almighty and the Lamb are its temple. The city does not need the sun or the moon to shine on it, for the glory of God gives it light, and the Lamb is its lamp. The nations will walk by its light and the kings of the earth will bring their splendor into it. On no day will its gates ever be shut, for there will be no night there. The glory and honor of the nations will be brought into it. Nothing impure will ever enter it, nor will anyone who does what is shameful or deceitful, but only those whose names are written in the Lamb's book of life. (Revelation 21:22-27)

Then, the angel showed me the river of the water of life, as clear as crystal, flowing from the throne of God and of the Lamb down the middle of the great street of the city. On each side of the river stood the tree of life, bearing twelve crops of fruit, yielding its fruit every month. And the leaves of the tree are for the healing of the nations. No longer will there be any curse. The throne of God and of the Lamb will be in the city, and his servants will serve him. They will see his face, and his name will be on their foreheads. There will be no more night. They will not need the light of a lamp or the light of the sun, for the Lord God will give them light. And they will reign forever and ever. (Revelation 22:1-5)

God is holy and majestic. May He be forever praised, and may He bless us all with eyes to see His glory and with hearts to worship His Son.

About the Author

F.B. Gold has held a variety of jobs: ranch hand, tree trimmer, medic in the US Army, and public-school teacher, coach, and counselor. He currently works in higher education. In his spare time, he enjoys exercising, playing golf, writing fiction and songs, and participating in Bible studies with his loved ones. His second published book is called, *To the Praise of His Glorious Grace: Weekly Reflections on God and His Word.* It can be found on Amazon. His prayer is that God would use his meager writings to expand His kingdom, by converting the unsaved of the world into committed worshipers of Christ, all for His glory.

Made in the USA
Columbia, SC
14 February 2025